reflection pond

I journey
bold and bright
make my bed by
Folding up the night

I sit on moon
and ponder stars
play my dreams
like lofty music bars

Kiss waking sun
who smiles and
walks with me

A Flower shy and bright
blossoms on the path
it wears my blushing face

I am Found
and home at last.

(Fictional child heart journal)

Reflection Pond

Jaiya John

Soul Water Rising

Silver Spring, Maryland

Printed in the United States of America

Soul Water Rising
Silver Spring, Maryland
http://www.soulwater.org

Library of Congress Control Number: 2007903754
ISBN 978-0-9713308-2-5

FIRST SOUL WATER RISING EDITION: 2007

Child & Youth Development

Editorial Team:
Jacqueline V. Richmond
Charlene R. Maxwell
Kent W. Mortensen

Cover design: R. Eric Stone
Whole identity graphic: R. Eric Stone

cherry blossom breaks free from bud
sky wraps her in its breezy bosom
sunlight frosts her silken skin
she is beauty born again.

a child is a poem learning to be beautiful

FIRST THOUGHTS

Revolutionary Indian leader Mohandas K. Gandhi wrote: *I have nothing new to teach the world. Truth and nonviolence are as old as the hills.* I also have nothing new to offer here. As it pertains to human nature, there are no new ideas, only fresh realizations of forgotten, neglected wisdom.

Most of what will cure our children's collective suffering is so natural we overlook its promise. An abundance of these remedies are found in the oral archives of our grandparent cultures. These are cultures that have largely been dehumanized and dismissed by *advanced* societies. The irony is that our predecessors long ago understood what we only now return to in dire need.

Millions of our world's children are forced through the curtain of separation from original family. The roster of causes is far too long: poverty, homelessness, abandonment, abuse, neglect, refugee status, immigration, parental mortality and incarceration, mental illness, addiction, juvenile transgression, war, child soldiering, child labor, sex slavery, epidemic, famine, natural disaster, genocide, and oppression.

While each experience is its own particularity, all such separations cleave the child heart and mind into a common root wound of vacancy and drift. Separation of course occurs in degrees. It can be permanent or temporary. Children can be separated from their entire family or from part of their family, such as from one parent or from siblings. Non-physical separation can occur even within the home, such as through the spirit-killing clouds of abuse and neglect. For all these reasons, it is fair to suggest that this story is the story of all children. Its focal point, however, is those young souls physically separated from their roots.

This book does not venture into the myriad causes of separation. It remains focused on the separation wound and its effects. It also addresses our relationship with these children as a function of our relationship with self. The way we embrace these children is a vital factor in their ultimate well-being. Our own woundedness is at play.

I envision *Reflection Pond* as a looking glass for all who raise or serve these youth. This includes expanded family (foster, adoptive, kin, guardian), educators, counselors, therapists, social service professionals, juvenile justice and legal authorities, legislators, mentors, and advocates.

These ideas are intended to inform legislation, policy, and practice; and to be a philosophical guide for our relationship with these youth. This book is not structured in traditional chapters. Instead, it is a single flow of brief meditative streams, each meant to create illumination for further personal growth and exploration. These short segments are meant to be easily digested and accessible, like inspirational thoughts returned to time and again.

My method has been to meditate on the thousands of children and youth I have met worldwide through my work and living. In those moments, I have been blessed in a priceless manner: These children have trusted me. Enough so that they opened up and revealed themselves to me. I believe that certain conditions created this sharing. The young people felt safe in the space we created together. They sensed they would not be judged, criticized, attacked, or betrayed.

They also deciphered that through my own separation, pain, healing, and growth, we somehow shared a common experience. From that commonality they seemed to feel I could relate to their reality *and* to the consequences of their reality. They could only sense these things in me because I offered to them the honest vulnerability of my childhood. I shared my stories with them before expecting them to share theirs with me.

Also, they could feel me *seeing* them. Not the masks they wore or the labels we have assigned them. They had nothing to hide because they saw in my eyes and felt in my energy that I had already discovered them and still felt admiration for who they truly were.

I do not claim any great insight. I only know that my heart is full, and that I have been led to share my inspiration. You will not find actual quotations from the children here, only my personal understanding of their true voice.

This book offers no rigid formulas or prescriptions. No how-to rules or top-10 lists. No undeviating notions or absolute knowledge. No magical promises or revelations. All this desperate clinging to ideas kills our spirit, stifles our creativity, dulls our divinely endowed intuition. This book is only a looking glass. We each must be the final author of our own expertise.

When we go looking for someone else to provide us with *the* final answer to our children's wellness, we insult our internal greatness. We sap our minds of imagination and our hearts of courage on our children's behalf. Worst of all, we become blind to the very child-truth we seek even as it stands before us in the flesh.

Belief itself can enslave us such that we refuse to depart the plantation of our conclusions. We refuse to leave even though our mental shackles cause us and others great suffering. We do not budge even as the stunted chain-length of those shackles prevents us from discovering the true child.

No child has ever existed entirely within the boundaries of the labels with which we seek to brand our young. In the end, ideas are no more than windows for us to pause before. We look *through* ideas on the chance we might catch a glimmer of a young life struggling to become. If we quest for her outside of our own instinct but inside our fearful sheath, we lose her. Finding her comes after letting go of what we *believe* we know. We were born with the ability to understand our children. Their nature is in us. Our great task is the unearthing. I pray that this story will bless the children whose lives we touch.

A FAWN'S STORY

Morning's air ushers the fawn shyly down the bank until she reaches water's edge. Her hooves sink into the mud as she extends herself toward the wavy sheen. She is still testing this place. Her eyes dart nervously around, peering into the surrounding forest, deciphering shapes, shadows, forms. Morning is quiet, calm. Her heartbeat is enormous. She has yet to determine whether she is safe here. Her life depends on it.

She looks into the water. It is resting. Clear enough to see through to the soft brown bottom. Motionless enough to provide her a certain comforting image: her own face takes form in the water. She is looking at herself. Relief rushes through her blood. Familiar things can calm the heart instantly. Her reflection leaves her feeling less alone, more assured.

A few moments of gazing at her face and surveying the water's perimeter are sufficient. She is safe enough to surrender some of her tension and taste what she thirsts for. Her lips touch down. The water is clear, cool, inviting. She is kissing her *self* as she drinks. The pond wears her face. She belongs here. Only leaves, breeze, and waves lapping shore are talking. She is safe. Her heartbeat slows further. Her muscles let go enough to receive the sustaining fluid.

Soon the sun will dance and demand the attention of every living thing. Heat will make Fawn its plaything, caging her up in its mouth, not releasing her until night shoos it away. She knows this is coming. It deepens her joy in this cool hour, at the edge of this tranquil mirror that shows her proof she is alive.

A good swallow of water causes Fawn to look up at the endless sky. White clouds that a few moments ago were light and laughing have darkened and gone morose. A breeze starts streaming. She feels the coming storm in her heart as her coat shifts, alert. A new conversation arises in the forest. This one sounds like Earth rolling over in its bed. Creatures are on the move.

Drops from the sky come down to meet their kin. Rain is a kind of cupid, bringing solitary water to the lover's ball that is a pond like this . . . *joining*. Sky-water touching Earth-water sews motion into the pond surface. Fawn is still thirsty, still frisky to play here in this spot that feels like home. Like all living things, she thrives in her relaxed state. But rain has kicked the water. Motion has stirred the pond floor into murky clouds. Between motion and pollution, Fawn's reflection disappears.

Her heartbeat is jogging again. Looking around the water and into the forest, Fawn is no longer so sure of what is and what isn't present here. The shapes in the shadows are shifting. Is a predator stalking her through the water curtain? Was that sound a branch snapping or teeth preparing? Fawn backs away from the water. She feels profoundly alone. None of her kind is here at all. This is the first moment she has realized this. None who looks like her. None who thinks like her. Not even one who moves like her. Clouds, trees, water—all of this used to be friendly in her eyes. Even related to her. Now she is in the presence of strangers.

When the first bolt strikes the forest, not 100 yards from her, all that is a stranger becomes her enemy. Earth shakes beneath her hooves. Her ground is not steady. Legs wobbling, she has lost all confidence in her abilities. The simplest thought or action overwhelms her. She half-forgets who she is. Her sense of self is running on waves of panic out of her body, racing to join the storm. She is quickly depleted. Adrenaline spasms her muscles but she has no direction, no guidance, no hint. So she runs in circles. For an endless moment, she darts aimlessly between water and trees. She finds no opening, no escape.

Although she cannot believe this, she is the very same fawn she was when the clouds were laughing. Only the world around her has truly changed. But she feels taken over inside, as though she has been replaced with this panicked amnesia. She does not remember herself; cannot retrieve her image from the water-mirror. Even this day's sunrise fades from her mind. She has lost possession of all things beautiful. She has lost her reflection pond.

THE NATURE OF REFLECTION PONDS

Born into this world, we humans are cast out from our mother's womb. We will spend our lives striving dearly, often desperately, to recreate the splendor of the womb. Those nearly 10 months of gestation were our grandest moment of security. We bathed in absolute warmth, nourishment, and comfort. Our truest needs were met. We knew we were not alone. At the breaching, we were expelled out into a stark reality of forms, light, and noise. The air temperature immediately chilled our skin.

This moment was the beginning of a questioning that would stay with us through our journey of life: *Who am I? Whose am I? Will my needs be met? If they are not, who will hear the cry of my suffering? Who will care among those who hear my cry? To whom am I beautiful? To whom am I worth this life of mine?*

On the breaking of our nascent moment of life our body is untethered from its formerly pregnant source. This unleashes throughout our being a deeply ingrained questioning of our own survival. Even as we bask in love and affection, the heart pulsing within us harbors a cavernous appetite for affirmation. Twin questions become our pulse: *Am I beautiful? Do I belong?*

When we receive human touch to our delicate skin we also receive a vital touch to our delicate sense of self. With each stroke we are penetrated yet farther with a belief that we exist. With each cry we send out, our well-being depends upon a kind return. We have already suffered our first primal separation—from the womb. Even in this budding infancy we are reckoning with a separation wound. The wound requires soothing. *Shhh, little baby, Mommy's here. Shhh, little darling, Daddy's going to make you feel all better. Shhh, little baby*—the reassuring voice we yearn for as long as we draw breath.

From the very beginning we are demanding of the world that cradles us: *I need to be held this way, fed this way, rocked to sleep this way; I need this kind of voice, these kinds of foods, this much sleep; I need this much quiet, this much attention, this temperature of bath water; I need the world to be this way.*

Our skill at communicating our needs increases rapidly. Our nature emerges accordingly. The failure to receive our needs and desires ignites a flame of doubt deep in our furnace: *If I am not receiving these things, does that mean something is wrong with me? Or that I do not belong with these people? Why am I being rejected?* Low self-regard is born easily on the shores of unfulfilling moments. A child's spirit is fragile sand eroded quickly by any sea that takes but does not give in the way her spirit requires.

To say that we are endlessly needy of the world's validation of us is not a criticism. It simply is our human nature. From kings in satin robes to monks in burlap robes, from elders in their wisdom cradle to babes in their dainty cradles, we are fundamentally and ceaselessly in need of validation.

Nature's primary mode of validating new life is to create it in the image of the life that precedes it. Plants, animals, water, earth, and humans—we all come forth in the image of that out of which we are born. This image has multiple dimensions. The fawn resembles the doe physically. Rain resembles the ocean chemically. One generation of baobab tree resembles its predecessors behaviorally. A child resembles her father or aunt temperamentally. A woman has a taste in food similar to her grandfather. A man has a taste in music reminiscent of his extended family.

Spiraling out from each of us into the realm of family, kinship, community, society, and ultimately humanity are concentric circles of relation. The closer a particular circle is to us, the more likely those in that circle are to share qualities with us. Farther out into the more distant orbits of life these affiliations or likenesses diminish. This is the pattern of existence itself. Planets closest to Earth's solar orbit are more likely to resemble the nature of Earth. Bodies within our galaxy will more often have familiar traits than will those bodies outside of our galaxy. In the great vortex of totality, physical proximity and biological kinship are both tied to similarity. This is not a law, but a pattern. And the pattern has a vital purpose.

Unlike most of nature, which goes about its existence without doubt-addled self-consciousness, we humans are strewn with second-guessing our own validity. A tree is blessed to live its life as a tree, not questioning whether it is as beautiful as a blade of grass, or as likeable as a mountain, or even as virtuous as the next tree over in the forest. Its life is fulfilled simply by being a tree.

We humans do not enjoy that simplicity. Especially those children separated from original family. Their wound opens a doorway into the possibility of their own inferiority. This doorway exists in each of us, but separation from original family as a child pries this opening much wider.

Reflection ponds are those parts of a child's social world that she can look into and see a reflection of herself. This reflection of the self can exist in many forms including: physical appearance; personality or nature; skills or talents; interests or inclinations; values and beliefs; social categories; and shared life experiences. Family, friendships, the school environment, the community, society, and humanity are all important potential reflection ponds. Virtually anything outside of the physical child, including her own creative works, can be a reflection pond. She can be her own reflection pond, if she is polished well enough.

When she looks into her father's face and sees her own, that is a reflection pond. It is telling her that she came from someone, something. This soothes her question of existence, a question that plagues her to a much greater degree than we may know.

When she enjoys the comfortable tranquility of a community she claims as her own, she is drinking from the replenishing waters of a reflection pond. Her people are a security net reveling in their unspoken and spoken shared values, desires, and experiences.

When she discovers a lifelong friend in college, at work, or elsewhere in the world—someone with whom she can get along and relate—she has stumbled upon a reflection pond. When someone *gets* her, and genuinely receives what she is sharing, that someone is her reflection pond. When her original family looks like her, and she is able to gaze upon them, she is gazing into her reflection pond. As she experiences her true self in any way, even in ways embroidered in pain, she is being blessed by the sustaining waters of a reflection pond.

The farther out from herself she travels in her concentric atmospheres, the less likely she will be to come upon a reflection pond. This is not absolute, it is a pattern. It is a tendency. Understanding tendencies can be useful in helping us co-construct her life in the way she needs it.

Reflection ponds are a fundamental building block for self-esteem, self-worth, and identity. They provide a child with a sense of belonging and beauty, and of purpose and promise. They foster feelings of safety and security in her, along with a role-modeling presence. They help her feel normal within family, community, and society. They provide a backdrop or measure of comparison for social and personal growth and development. They validate her uniqueness and sameness, and instill confidence, hope, and a sense of possibility.

We must remind ourselves why we toil and what is at stake when the words *cultural integrity* escape our lips. When the words *child welfare* slip from our tongue. At the core of all this noise generated by adults there stands, vulnerable and frightened, the child, unsure of who she is to these people called family and community. Uncertain of her place in this world, she looks for evidence that she is real. She does so by scanning the faces around her, hoping to see the slightest physical resemblance. She listens on a level we have long forgotten, to hear the rhythm, tone, voice, vibration that feels good to her, somehow natural to her. She looks to the canvass that is her humanity and hopes to find the portrait composed of lines and angles that make sense to her, soothing her soul to sleep at night.

Eager perspiration falls
from her smooth face
as she plays with abandon
always fearing deep inside
abandonment
by those adults around her
who seem to forget how much
it meant as a child
to be wrapped in the cocoon
of similarity familiarity
and family even if imperfect
even if faded into the final acres
of her togetherness

togetherness
the land she desperately
cultivates inside her memories.

A child wanders a canyon that is her family, her world.
She shouts out, waits for the echo. The echo says: *We have
heard you, we have understood you. We care enough to attempt
to replicate your shout/whistle/song and give it back to you,
with the same vibration, pitch, resonance.* This is your
evidence that you belong to us, are a part of us.

Why does she shout into the canyons of her life? The
echo is evidence that she is valid. That she belongs. That
she exists. Belongingness (connectedness) is the primal
pulse that drives her existence from conception to birth to
the end of her days. In this sense, attachment is very much
a dynamic of spirituality or life force. That is, at her core
essence, an energy drive exists that inherently seeks to
manifest and exercise her attachment to the world.

She is an echo walker, boomerang thrower, constantly
tossing her essence against the wind. She needs it to reach
her world, and be returned to her relatively unchanged.

Anxiety fuels her constant testing. Change stokes the fuel into fire. She sips her safety from the reflection ponds in her life: family, community, society. When those reflection ponds grow murky, she loses confirmation of herself and of her place within those ponds.

GATHERING REFLECTION PONDS

Just as a body of water must be clear and still to provide us a reflection of our own physical appearance, reflection ponds in a child's life require similar traits. The relationship between a child and a particular reflection pond must contain stillness: consistency and stability. Clearness—honesty and effective communication—is also imperative between the two.

Something within the reflection pond must be similar to, or in harmony with, something within the child. When a child looks into or experiences the reflection pond, she should feel that sense of harmony, understanding, or similarity. She should immediately experience positive and affirming sensations, feelings, or thoughts. Certainly the reflection pond must be accessible to her so that she can regularly draw forth her own reflection.

We become a reflection pond to a child when we listen compassionately and truly receive what she shares with us. When she can witness what she has shared taking root in us, flowering, we become her reflection. When her beauty blossoms all around our home, not just in her bedroom, we transform into her reflection. When she notices that we talk about and ask about the things and people she cares about, we are transformed in her eyes. As she notices change in us that mirrors traits in her, she sees herself in us and is comforted.

She acquires reflection ponds when she feels safe in her community: safe from prejudice, spotlights, and subtle tensions; when her extended family and society show a comfort with the traits that make her special. When she sees how her nature is a reflection of the nature of the trees, water, sky, Earth, and animals around her.

She is rich in reflection ponds when *where* she comes from and *who* she comes from are celebrated. A displaced child cannot feel whole if her new family or community is rejecting her parts.

When she is taught that her dreams are real and possible, her very dreams become a reflection pond. She can see herself in a healthy marriage. She can see herself being a successful educator or global leader. We humans require the ability to literally see our face inhabit distant social realities in order to muster the will and courage to span those distances. Most of all, we must realize that our ability to reflect *her* back to her is largely a function of our own personal and collective growth in her direction.

THREATS TO REFLECTION PONDS

A reflection pond is as fragile in its effectiveness as a body of water is vulnerable to being stirred up and made unclear. Dishonesty between us and children is a destructive force that clouds our shared reflection pond. We are often dishonest with uprooted children about the special nature of biological relationships. We do this to protect their hearts, given their disconnection from family. More often than not, this dishonesty backfires. Their whole life they see the world around them, including us, celebrating biological connections. Instead of dishonesty, we can explain the unique value and frequency of non-biological relationships. This honesty will go a long way toward creating a clear reflection.

Our prejudice toward dislocated children may be the most damaging threat to our own reflective quality. Prejudice (negative, dehumanizing judgments lacking complete information) dispels reflection ponds. When children are exposed to prejudice targeting their traits, character, and life, they lose a sense of beauty and belonging. Children can sense even subtle parental prejudice or negative feelings and attitudes. This leaves children scalded by the very people from whom they need the most absolute embrace of love and affection.

Modern racial prejudice is subtle rather than blatant. This means that much of the prejudice children are exposed to from family, extended family, and community is often difficult for others to notice or define. This includes the perpetrators themselves. As a result, children are too often left to manage for themselves how to deal with, discuss, and heal from these hurtful attitudes. Their identity, attachment, esteem, and overall development are thus compromised.

Many other threats to reflection ponds exist. Lack of social diversity within an environment makes it more likely that youth will fail to see themselves in that potential reflection pond. Children who feel they are not truly listened to, understood, or validated lose to a great extent the benefit of their own reflection in the world around them.

Anything that creates inconsistency, instability, or unpredictability in a relationship can disrupt the reflective quality of that relationship. Children's perceived lack of safety in any environment diminishes that environment's reflective quality. Harsh tones of voice, control impulses, condescending attitudes, anger, abuse, manipulation, deceit, non-communication—all of these dynamics coming from others can impact children's ability to derive their own reflection from those people.

Reflection ponds are dissipated when we fail to honor children by seeing the truth within them and within their lives. Among the most important truths we need to recognize are the wounds uprooted children often carry.

WOUND OF SEPARATION

Separation from original family is a moment that fertilizes a child forever with the realistic possibility that she may be separated again—from original family or from anyone else with whom she dares to join her heart.

Her mental receptor cells transform through this trauma and become immediately more proficient at receiving and processing the possibility of future separations, future aloneness. This is the mechanical aspect of an essential change in her identity: *I have been separated. Separation is a part of who I am. Separation may very well follow me.*

An intrinsic wound lives within separation. If we cut off a finger we will bleed. It does not matter how unsightly, misshapen, disabled, or dysfunctional our finger was before we cut it off. If we cut it off, we bleed. This is the nature of things when parts of us are severed from our being. These natural laws do not change. The same is true of a child's attachments. When he loses them, he bleeds. How we feel about his original family is irrelevant.

To honor the child we are required to honor his family, kin, and community. We have to honor the fact that in having those roots severed from him, he bleeds. Whether or not we feel those roots are worth bleeding over. And regardless of the age at which he is separated.

We do not get to choose whether a child bleeds, just as we do not get to choose whether in losing our finger we bleed.

Human beings do not exist in a void unattached to our past or to the life embedded within us. This notion is the offspring of cultural ideas of independence, individualism, freedom, and self-determination. All worthy notions, each of which, when taken too far or out of context, results in an unnatural relationship with life and the world. As with all of life, imbalance eventually creates chaos and distress.

Nestled between the fanciful absolutes of singularity and commonality is the far meadow toward which we trek. There, roots are honored, past is revered, personal possibility is venerated. The child's entirety is bowed down to in humble deference. Each of his shepherds is aware that to be made a shepherd is to be blessed with the enormity of leading without possessing; guiding without controlling; polishing without tarnishing; supporting without suffocating.

Inherently, separation from original family involves a rupturing or disappearance of nature's primary reflection pond. A child's positive sense of her self in the world has begun to drain out through the crevasse of this separation. She may be largely unaware of this seepage, but she feels its outflow in the form of anxiety, fear, doubt—an unsettling sensation of having the Earth pulled out from under her feet. Nothing feels solid any longer.

It is hard to exist securely in such a reality. What to us may seem like the smallest of things can rear itself as a humongous uncertainty to this child: *Will (new) Dad's disappointment with me today mean he will reject me tomorrow, once he thinks about it some more? I missed that free throw in the basketball game. Will my friends stop liking me?* The parade of doubtful, fearful thoughts can quickly become a waterfall carrying a child far away from peace.

The wound of separation brings pain and challenges even when a child has been separated from an unhealthy circumstance. In fact, any unhealthy circumstance plays a relatively small role in the magnitude of the separation wound a child ultimately experiences.

Separation from the original root can override in significance the dysfunctions involved with that root. As a society we often underestimate this truth. We assume that because we have *rescued* a child from a horrible reality that the child's path should be smoother from here on out. Instead, the child now must contend with the wounds born of her separation as well as those born of her exposure to dysfunction. This is not an argument against separation. It is an acknowledgement of the child's truth.

Suddenly she is alone and drifting in the world; her well-being in the hands of people she may not know at all. Abandonment is not at the core of her separation wound. Separation is. Thoughts of abandonment are secondary to the acute impact of realizing *I am without my family or a part of my family. I may never see them again.* The child's heart now is a vase breaking over and over with every repetition of these thoughts, like a nightmare that refuses to bid her farewell.

Often we believe that if we simply place a child in the hands of a new, loving caregiver, this should be the recipe for the child's healing. But her heart has been turned to shards by her separation. Until this is addressed, her healing cannot be complete. A new parent cannot replace the meaning of a previous one, especially an original one. Realizing the impact of the child's separation is important. If we misidentify the nature of her wound, we are prone to frustration at any lack of her healing and growth.

This absence of original family can rain down violently and without compassion on a young mind. It can be a relentless taunting truth: *I am away from my home. I am away from my father, my sisters and brothers. I am not complete.* Each day she wakes and is visited by the same reality again. The coldness of this circumstance can cause her to detach from the world. She does not know how to be herself in a world without her family. So she becomes shy and withdrawn at being in the world at all. She is a baby turtle pulling back into its shell.

No one has prepared her for this journey. The adults who seek to guide her have mostly not ventured this way themselves. She feels blind and as though she is being led by the blind. Good intentions are all around her and yet she feels virtually unattended.

Her self-regard is sand pouring through the hourglass with each moment she is away from her root. Even as she begins to enjoy the benefits that may come from a more stable environment, there is a hole in her spirit through which her essential sand is escaping. This hole can only be plugged by efforts that directly affirm her actual connection and belonging to her source. Although she has been torn from her root, her root still lives in her. She still lives in her root. This story must be relentlessly repeated to her and activated in her own mind and actions. It cannot be repeated too much. It must become a mantra: *I am of my root. My root is of me. We can never truly be divided. We shall feed each other forever.*

A child does not only experience a personal wound in the midst of separation. She also internalizes the wound her original family suffers in losing her. This is not her imagination. She truly feels their loss, takes it in, and makes it a part of her wound. Just as we suffer in empathy at sadness in those close to us, a child suffers knowingly of the loss her family endures. Those she is separated from always grieve losing her. Their flaws, indiscretions, and failures do not change this.

When a tree is torn from the Earth, the Earth mourns along with the tree. Not only that, the tree is forever haunted by the Earth's mourning. A separated child is not simply imagining that her family must be mourning. She feels the wave of mourning. It reaches her wherever she is; no matter how well she is doing; no matter how we dress her in clothes, education, and opportunity.

In helping her heal, we contend with a mix of wounds. Some come from her original family and some originate in her. All are valid. Questioning the validity of a wound is nearly meaningless and ultimately counterproductive to her healing. Not to mention to her relationship with we who claim to be there for her.

Remember your childhood security blanket, favorite doll, cherished secret hiding place? Remember what they meant to you then? How you longed for them when they were no longer present? Magnify this aching need by the intensity of a thousand sunsets. This is the importance of original family to children, no matter a family's character or impact on its young. Families too often hurt children. This is known. Making judgments of those crimes and failings does not help a child heal and grow. Like athletes in training, we must visualize and constantly remind ourselves that what matters is the nature of the separation wound. Beyond that, our focus is on our options for facilitating a child's journey toward health.

We are not addressing here the relative goodness of various families, only the indescribable importance nature has rendered into families for every child. Our focus must remain on these core truths. We should work hard at avoiding the temptation to judge, scorn, blame, and dehumanize a child's roots. Our place is as the shepherd to the lost lamb. Her heart's yearning is not so much a function of the character of her first flock, but of her dire need to be a beautiful part of that flock.

Separation from at least part of the original family is the experience of millions of the world's children. This frequency alone bears our close attention. We cannot afford to underestimate the internal disruption caused by the absence of one parent even as the other remains, or by the loss of a sibling.

Children are even more often torn from extended family, with real consequences. Extended family in many cases includes people who have parental or at least very close relationships with these children. Kinship is so essential a feature in many cultures that the delineation between nuclear and extended family is nonexistent. Blood relation not being a requirement of kinship, the family circle from which many children are torn can easily consist of dozens of members. Separation from parts of this familial fold can render deep wounds of the same nature as those caused by separation from an entire family.

Separation does not visit an individual child alone, in a vacuum. It visits her generations as a cycle of separation. It creates an internal poverty that itself becomes a cycle. This cruel vortex generally spins through a series of stages, within her life and across generations: disruption, separation, internal crisis, external manifestation, institutionalization, systemic illness, marginalization and death, and finally, absence from succeeding generations.

We can visualize this cycle as a flowing stream. For each child caught in the stream's current, entry points exist at which we can reach him. Sometimes this flow is circular more than it is linear. The nature of the stages or entry points is what we should focus on. Each introduces a child to new wounds and challenges. Each offers us unique opportunities to intervene. No static blueprint exists for what these stages hold. But if we view them as an interconnected body we are afforded better insight—into the phenomenon of separation and into each child.

WOUND OF ISOLATION

Social realities in this world dictate that children separated from original family tend to fall into two distinct and significant cultural flows or drifts: The flow into isolation away from one's heritage, and the flow from material poverty class into material comfort class.

Social power dictates child flows. Children separated from original family tend to be pitched into these two strong currents. Without judging, we can imagine that this alone might create a sense of isolation for children, beyond that of being apart from family.

Social power groups have a dominant say-so regarding our global reaction to children in crisis, children who end up carried away from original family. These youth have moved away from not only family, but also from the familiarity and cultural continuity of their past. Our temptation is to cheer this movement and say *What a wonderful blessing for those children. They come from people and places that are not fit for children.*

We must be careful in our cheering. Isolation, in any form, can be the most dehumanizing and defeating experience of all. When we separate children not only from their original root but also from their broader cultural nests, the effects can be subtle, insidious, and exponential. Not because cultural realities should be considered exclusive determinants of a child's life, but because these isolating factors can have a critical impact on well-being. Our mainstream biases lean us toward valuing the extraction of children from certain communities. Following these biases faithfully does not mean we best serve children. Like all of us, children dwell in a life cloud of relativity. We often assign value to the character of their families and communities in comparison to other families and communities. But children's sense of wellness is first derived from their perceived beauty and belonging among *their* people. Moving a child from a materially lacking community to a community thriving in resources can be as traumatic to her as moving her in the other direction. This may be hard for us to believe if we have not ourselves endured such dislocation. This is why the voices that matter authoritatively are those of dislocated children.

Even as we praise the movement of a child out of a war-stricken, child-soldiering reality into a *stable, civilized* environment, we must be careful. This new environment can create new, meaningful wounds in the child simply by virtue of the extreme sense of isolation.

Isolation causes the soul to question its very existence. Isolation harasses the soul ceaselessly. It is a voice in the head spiraling the child down into a steadily decaying identity: *You are not the same as them. You are not the same. You are not as good. You are not as good. There is something wrong with you. There is something wrong. You do not belong. You do not belong. If you do not belong here, you may not belong anywhere. You may not belong.*

Isolation over time is not a single raindrop falling for a billion years onto a rock, carving it slowly. It is an immediate assertive criticism of personhood. Even truly secure children quickly lose hold on the cliffs of isolation. When they are cast into isolation, the wound of separation mutates into a dual storm that batters even children seeking refuge in *civilized* places.

In isolation, a child's powerful drive for positive sameness slams against a hard wall of difference. The child then experiences an *otherness* or outsider-self in relation to his world. All his positive attributes mean little to him if he is surrounded by people who appear to be part of a group that he is not. The beautiful soul standing outside on the doorstep of the party does not feel beautiful at all.

A lazy validation comes from being part of the norm. We all fall prey to looking down upon those who deviate from our perch of normalcy. We say to ourselves: *Most of the people around me believe as I do, see things as I do, experience life as I do. So this person who is different from us, her feelings and perceptions are suspect. I don't see enough people supporting her way of being, so she must be wrong.*

An isolated child feels this stream of deduction running through his peers. He naturally fights to contradict the mass opinion in defense of his experience. But mass opinion and perspective have a way of wearing down isolated souls. The drowned-out child stops trying to represent his own truth. He adopts the stance of the masses. He abandons himself. Or grows angry and revolts.

This of course is not tolerated by the masses. Mainstream grows quickly offended when it is contradicted, especially in anger. Now the isolated child is branded with labels such as *troublemaker, rebel, malcontent, bitter.* Whatever words can be used to paint the offending child into a corner of shame and marginality are slathered on, whitewashing away his vital distinctions.

Many children are heritage or cultural tokens in their new family or community. They are extremely isolated numerically from those with whom they share a particular root. Those who have not experienced this kind of extreme marginalization may be tempted to minimize its impact. Yet its damaging effects have been well documented for decades. For children in the bright lights of standing out, even popularity is potentially damaging. Heightened focus on them, whether positive or negative, can disrupt their growth and pierce their sense of safety. The more emotionally charged the distinctive trait, the more potent and virulent the isolation or tokenism. Prejudice, physical distinctiveness, and intergroup history are among the seeds for this potency. Most children who have been separated from original family experience some degree of tokenism. Their separation status alone is enough to create the isolation.

Being a token can exact a tremendous toll on children's self-esteem, learning, overall health, and social interactions. It can damage their relationships, sense of belonging and beauty, and their degree of eventual life success. The sojourn out of this solitary valley can take a lifetime. A great deal of the time, this sojourn involves navigating life's mainstreams.

MAINSTREAMS

Invisible affirmations come to those who belong to the mainstream. Those not of the mainstream but who choose or are forced to swim in it do get wet, do receive some kind of reward for their obedience. But never do they fully become that main water. Never do they reap the fullness of its affirmations. For those gifts are showered only upon those who belong.

We are not giving something extra to side-stream children. We are giving them what mainstream children receive invisibly. Because of that invisibility, what is provided to children outside the norm seems to be a special consideration. An *invisible massage* or stroking occurs for those within the norm. We must be persistent in asking:

What affirming actions are we taking on behalf of the child who exists outside the mainstream? She swims virtually alone.

Those who swim in the mainstream of any cultural dimension are very aware of the biases in their favor. They feel guilt and shame over this. They desire to see their life as being entirely the result of personal character and not of social benefits handed down through a history of inequity. They have something to aid their denial of privilege: Invisibility.

Mainstreams by nature are invisible to those who swim in them. Such people's *way of being* is so dominant in a given environment that over time it becomes accepted as simply *being normal*. Those who swim there often fail to see that their way is a cultural way. Instead they view it as a personal way. Because so many others emulate their personal way, and because that way is the endorsed way of being and seeing, they are personally validated: they are *superior, civilized, advanced.* The cultural aspect of their nature is so taken for granted as individual normalcy that they become blind to it. They begin to say things like: *I wish I had a culture.*

As those in any mainstream deny the cultural influence on their *personal way,* their culture disappears into the fabric of their life. Through this denial, those who swim in the mainstream see those who swim in side streams as deviations from normalcy and therefore inherently inferior. Mainstream exerts a powerful force. Those in the side streams are expected to vacate their ways and join the main group.

The biting chagrin of the mainstream is that they do not get to be the ultimate authority on the insults suffered by side streams. They try dearly. They say to side streams: *I understand your experience. I've experienced the same thing in my own way. Let's stop dividing ourselves and come together.*

The whisper woven into their words: *Come join our stream. Your stream frightens us.* This is the psychology of oppression and the death of children from *other* streams.

Numerical or power dominance creates the illusion of superiority. This harms those in the mainstream and those in the side streams. The mainstream goes through life blinded with a false sense of self, one bridled with notions of being at the center of the world. Side streams go through life also blinded. Theirs is a false sense of inferiority, an absence of self-permission to *be*. Neither stream can truly know itself within this illusion. A quest awaits them before they can see their true place and value within the world. Before they can see each other clearly.

Children whose heritage or culture carries them outside of the mainstream swim a peculiar current. Swimming against the grain creates an inherent friction and tension. Mundane daily existence requires more effort. Those in the mainstream are largely blinded to their own ease of movement and to the obstructed movement of these youth. This blindness is perhaps most harmful of all.

A side-stream child becomes *the boy who cried wolf* as he contends with the myth of multiculturalism. A society is not multicultural as long as its dominant culture is unwilling to honestly question and challenge its past and present impact on others. This denial and avoidance leave side-stream youth under constant, unnoticed assault.

Mainstream culture is not likely to see itself as a culture at all, but simply as people being people. Everyone else is labeled as marginal, minority, ethnic, cultural, exotic, mysterious, under-developed, third world, uncivilized, disadvantaged. Everyone else is *Other*. There can be no true multiculturalism under these conditions. The mainstream sees itself as being *above culture*. It dismisses side stream calls for its heritage and culture to be honored. Side-stream children continue being battered by domination waves.

Mainstream is a force that can say one thing and mean another. Its claims of multiculturalism seem to be saying: *Let's all come together and create something new and better.* But a truer meaning may be: *Let's all come together and play under our mainstream cultural rules.* This is not an indictment. It is the nature of mainstreams. Perpetuation of dominant power is our human temptation. But this attitude is not multiculturalism, it is cultural babysitting. It is flirtation with respect for others.

When we babysit, we welcome another's child; but when that child does not behave according to the rules of the house, we sanction the child. What's more, we feel this house to still be *our* house, not a place equally endowed to both us and the child. Most crucial of all, we engage in the relationship as parent-to-child, with all the attendant paternalism, condescension, and control. This may be acceptable when literally babysitting a child. But when raising, mentoring, educating, or otherwise embracing a displaced child, he must be held in relative equity. Any hurtful friction between his ways and ours needs to be held in full light and addressed with sincerity.

WOUND OF STIGMA

We commonly look upon separation from family, regardless of cause, as indicative of a flaw in the child. Separation is not just noticeable, it is a stigma. Stigma is a seed for shame, inferiority, self-blame for circumstance, and social isolation.

Stigma can prevent a child from engaging in necessary healing. She may believe she does not deserve to heal, and that she does not deserve happiness. Stigma creates a wall between the child and her community, a segregation that further drives esteem downward.

Perhaps most of all, stigma prevents and short circuits the vital relationships a child requires within her social world in order to exercise her humanity. Knowing that she is perceived as somehow broken or flawed, a child is less likely to assert her true beauty into her environment. She may hide her true self and engage in mimicry and imitation of others to gain approval. She will bloody herself banging on the door of acceptance trying to get in.

She may also respond to this stigmatization by creating a shell of silence around her wounds as well as around the beauty in her personality. Feeling as though she is being viewed critically, she may decide she cannot trust anyone with her heart.

Stigma also causes children who share similar separation wounds from discovering each other. They keep their stories hidden and in doing so make it harder to find one another in the community or world. They amplify their foreboding sense of aloneness. This is the irony of their protective secrecy.

We can encourage these children to express their stories in safe, comfortable ways. We can help them to develop the skills necessary for this storytelling. In doing this, we equip them with a capacity for healing and growing. Beyond all external interventions, children ultimately must gain the tools for their own determination. When children learn to assert their truth they dislodge the teeth of social stigma. They make people see their beauty.

Prejudice is at the root of the stigma of separation and feeds upon shared ignorance. Gossip and whispers gain momentum like a fireplace stoked by bellows. Even within a child's new family, people pass on to each other their uninformed ideas about what the child must be thinking and feeling; and what horrors she came through. The stories are repeated until they are held as truth.

It is difficult enough for children to trust people not familiar with their experience. When they sense those people's prejudice toward them, trust is almost impossible. We cannot fairly expect children to feel safe and secure when they are thrust into families and communities dripping with prejudice toward them.

The ludicrous nature of our expectations turns yet crueler when we then criticize these children for not accepting our love and embrace. How could they? Our love is tainted and our embrace is false.

WOUND OF FALSE EMBRACE

We believe we are embracing uprooted children with everything they need, short of their original family. In fact, much of what we embrace them with is our own wounds, fears, insecurities, and expectations. These elements are born of our life experiences and cultural realities. We should be careful to see these children for who they are and to listen to them compassionately. If not, we risk the danger of bringing into their lives harmful elements along with our more positive contributions.

Looking deeply into a child requires intensive self-awareness. This awareness takes work but it cannot be avoided. We should ask ourselves: *What is the full inventory of what I am bringing into this child's life?* Are we bringing a need to control along with our stable home, material wealth, and education? Are we bringing a deep, unrecognized prejudice toward this child's cultural heritage along with our parenting skills? This is an inventory that must be taken. When we discover potentially harmful elements in our basket there is no need to run away screaming. We need only stop and make a commitment to clean those elements from our store.

Prejudice cannot hide. No manner of costume, makeup, or mask we may adorn to disguise ourselves from a child is powerful enough to conceal our prejudices. In the end we seed her with that painful contradiction of aversion living in the place where love should be.

Our young catch the minutest flickers of muscle in our faces. Our body language, which we feel is subtle, is a theatrical giveaway. They know exactly what discomforts us and how much those things discomfort us. Our prejudice and fear are bright colors we weave on the loom. We have no choice but to admit these things and go about transforming our anxiety into ease. Our relationship with the child will make the same transition: anxiety into ease. Flickering faces always give away our true hearts.

Cultural blindness is a potent threat to children. If we are unable to engage in a committed journey into the cultural reality of a child, how can we say that we understand the needs of the child? How can we be aware when we are bruising her heart, or further hampering her growth toward self-love? Sensitivity is not something we conjure up by desire. It is a capacity to *know* the child that we acquire through work, over time, and with humility.

There is no human being who is not entirely cultural. Every aspect of our existence is cultural. Pure individualism is a myth. There is a cultural root to our ideas, our feelings, our reactions, our values, and our ways. Accept this and the next thing we realize is that our cultural vision leaves us with blind spots in accurately perceiving the child. She is a product of her cultural reality. To judge her personality, strengths, and challenges through the prism of our cultural vision is to presume that she has no validity outside of our cultural reality. She feels this as a daily ill wind.

False embrace comes when we feel we are giving the child a tonic and she only grows sicker. Then upon proper examination, we discover that what we believed was a tonic, for her was poison. What is medicine to us may very well be toxic to this particular child. We cannot know this until we have at least made the effort to know. Homework is a concept we expect our children to embrace. How many of us actually embrace life's truest homework, the devoted study of another human being in the context of who she is and what her life has been?

The false embrace that so often greets our youth imbues them with the piercing conflict of love and prejudice in the same hearts: the hearts of those who care for them, teach them, befriend them. We speak of love as though we who possess it are chivalrous perfection, as though our love means we are void of harmful essence.

But prejudice is a common bedfellow to love. We may love our young dearly and yet carry a profound prejudice toward much of what they represent. Their faces, bodies, behavior, speech, ways of being, circumstances, and heritage can all be triggers for negative associations we make with certain groups of people. These ideas are socialized into us from birth. Repeated exposure imbeds this negativity deeply in us. Our love for children, by itself, may do little to dissolve these powerful links.

A deep pain visits children who are placed in an environment in which they taste, smell, and see this contradiction daily. They have no choice but to try and bond with and trust those in their life. But it is those very people from whom they detect a hurtful reaction to parts of who they are. They are stuck. They are expected to be grateful for all the love they are being given. And they are.

But peace eludes them because they also swallow a steady stream of negative pulses. It is in the air around them like an electrical field. They feel it in the home, at school, in the streets. Their own society shoots it at them through the television and motion picture screens. They are a target. How do they gain a foothold on this wicked slope? How do they begin to feel safe here, with these people whose own hearts are divided?

The responsibility is ours to clean out our hearts when we bring a child into our space. Who invites children over to play and has artwork all over the house depicting monsters eating children? We do. We do this when we invite a child into our lives without making the effort to clean out the garbage of prejudice that has accumulated in us through our years.

The paradox of love and prejudice grows more prevalent the more unfortunate a child's life has been. Tragedy pastes stigma on a child's forehead. Stigma attracts prejudice like decay attracts birds of prey. The more we love, the more painful it is for us to admit our prejudices toward the children we love. We have no choice. This bittersweet potion we offer is killing the relationship. It is killing peace.

HERITAGE AND CULTURE

Heritage is the life we have inherited, all of that essence poured into us at conception and throughout life. Culture is the life we have made. Heritage is the ocean within us. Culture is the mist rising from that ocean. It is made of the ocean and yet it is more. It is our flowering into the world, our extension beyond the vital foundation. Culture is our *way of being*, a mist revelation born from our mixing of ocean (heritage), wind (life), and air (self). We dare imagine what might be beyond what has been, yet even in our flight toward that dream our path and speed are the offspring of the ocean. This glorious mist is culture.

Because culture is literally *the way in which a person exists in the world*, there is an inherent and powerful link between a child's culture and her state of health. To the degree that her personal culture is not understood, supported, and incorporated, her capacity to process life is in danger of being overburdened. Health is a holistic personal system that involves emotions, cognition, and spirit or vitality as much as it involves the body. Compromises to any aspect of a child's health ultimately affect her total health. Culture is a brilliant constellation of lights within us, each sparkling to the degree the others shine. Our health resides in this delicate chandelier.

Heritage matters more than ever. It provides an ancestral, social embrace for isolated children. It is a security blanket and a pacifier. Heritage is a source portrait that lends location and orientation to a spinning youthful top. The more the world grows in population and social complexity, the more children need roots to anchor and steady them.

A strong sense of heritage hooks children up to an incredible power source. This can make them feel bigger than their pain, stronger than those who hurt them, more formidable than their separation from family. Their inherited power source can allow them to withstand the hurt and come out intact.

Heritage is not just a story to be told. It is a living receptacle of wisdom accumulated over the course of hundreds of lifetimes. Heritage is the cup of wisdom. If heritage were so meaningless, why is it the first possession that oppressors seek to steal from a people? Any strong and healthy community celebrates and preserves its heritage as a matter of survival.

Mainstreams repeatedly try to convince side streams that heritage is divisive and to be transcended. Mainstreams know that a side stream who clearly knows itself is empowered beyond the reach of domination. Such a stream cannot be oppressed. Mainstreams know this because they celebrate and preserve their heritage relentlessly. It keeps them aloft in the world. Mainstreams are often threatened by side streams in touch with their heritage. This is because heritage is a guidebook detailing survival strategies in the midst of mainstreams.

A child is a civilization unto herself. To the extent that she drinks from the accumulated wisdom of her lineage she is rich, rooted, and sturdy. To the degree she fails to drink this tonic of her ages, she is a brilliant book made brittle by her non-acquaintance with her own pages.

The whole point of generations is for their mettle to be made, then to be passed down. Our dear child, she is a lagoon at the foot of a waterfall. If our impulse is to enslave her spirit, we need only dam to a halt the flow of her waterfall. If we dream of her as a vital source for things that grow from her lagoon, we will allow her generations to complete their fall into her waters.

WHOLE IDENTITY

Chief Seathl (Seattle) spoke these words: *Humankind has not woven the web of life. We are but one thread within it. Whatever we do to the web, we do to ourselves. All things are bound together. All things connect.*

Life waits for its many creations to recognize each other as siblings. When we do, all struggle dissolves. Struggle is only here in the first place because we fail to recognize we actually *are* each other. When our children realize and then activate their meaningful relationship or oneness with all aspects of their world, they become whole. When they begin to experience even apparently unrelated parts of the world as internal, personal experiences, they are becoming whole.

When children believe those they are in conflict with are an extension of themselves, they are achieving wholeness. When they realize that they cannot afford to hurt even those who are hurting them, they have reached an advanced state of wholeness.

Whole identity is the act of dissolving into the world. In this state, we no longer hold tight to the idea of a separate self. This is our truest exhale. We become all things. We feel a sensation similar to orchestra members in peak harmony or athletic teammates in a magical groove, operating at their highest level. We can feel our teammates' pulse, we are so in synch. This is whole identity. We have surrendered our separateness and drowned into everything. The past, present, and future are revealed for their true circular nature—one that revolves in our every moment; each a piston firing into the revolution.

When a leaf shifts in the wind and we feel the shift in our heart, this is our wholeness speaking. When every human pain and joy that ever was becomes a concert in our heart, we are whole. When we recognize the ancestors walking by our side even as we smile upon our distant descendants, we are whole. When those who hurt us become in our mind the challenging variation of those who protect us, we are supremely whole. The optimal state for children, and for us, is waiting in this totality.

WHOLE IDENTITY GRAPHIC: Whole identity is achieved when a child sees all aspects of her world as being an actual, meaningful part of her. She recognizes and activates the oneness of life and her vital place in this web. Each aspect within her whole is an element of her personal culture, her *way of being*. She has a relationship with each aspect. The health of each relationship defines her degree of wholeness.

Each element in the graphic presented here is a pool of the child's essence overflowing into the others. A sense of positive connectedness in one life area feeds her well-being in other life areas. When she experiences disconnection or harm in any area, all other areas are affected. Her wellness ripples back and forth through these pools, her cultural web. Each pool is a potential reflection pond for her. This graphic represents only some of the vast number of life elements that compose her whole.

When children have a fractured vision of self, when they believe they are apart from the world, they are vulnerable as babes left out in the snow. This self-portrait of a drifting, disconnected soul leads to harmful and self-destructive attitudes, choices, and actions. Such youth feel they have no place in the world. They suffer a perceived and continual rejection by the world. Their moments are bloated with redundant mental lashings, emotional self-mutilation, ceaseless punishing thoughts of banishment.

So destructive is a fractured identity that a focus on instilling and preserving youths' sense of whole identity is at the core of our global possibility: securing the future of our generations.

In that culture is the substance of life—values, beliefs, worldviews, inclinations, rhythm, vision, etc.—all aspects of whole identity are by definition cultural identity. This is an invaluable insight into the needs and modes of resolution for child crises. Cultural tapestry can be used as a tool for exploring the roots of disruption and as a device for discovering appropriate healing and stabilizing factors.

Whole identity represents not the life categories with which we associate, but the nature of our relationship with those categories. Identity is a warm-blooded phenomenon of attitudes, particularly those anchored in love and affection, and prejudice and aversion. Both streams are processes of bias shaping our perception of the world and ourselves. Both streams feed into prejudices that can prevent our beliefs from maturing and evolving. Identity is a sensational boilerplate that overwhelmingly shapes how children, and we, exist in the world.

SURRENDERING TO THE LARGER SELF

Our children's lives wear the clothing of many helpers and yet on the inside they walk alone. Is this not just a sharper form of every human journey? Surrounded by so many, and yet in the breast of every moment, if we look with courage, we see that our most intimate truth is ours alone. This can horrify the most grounded of us. Comfort comes only when we adopt a way of looking that brings the world as it truly is into our spirit home. Children require this same way of looking, this vision that recognizes the larger play unfolding in their lives.

Children need our help to release their entrenched notions of separateness and surrender to the truth that the world is within them. This is a grand step, a vital clause in the agreement between children and peace . . . opening up their flow channels and allowing all of life to flood into their being—what an ecstatic shower. What an enormous drowning. Children can enjoy the simultaneous truth of their soul journey this way—both singular and collective; both solitary and joined by everything and everyone.

This great opening into a whole identity brings everything that was ever beautiful into children's being. They have no hope then of not feeling beautiful; not thinking beautiful; not being beautiful. All the smiling faces of their life join them; all the compassion and kindness join them; all the glory of the natural world reveals itself as buds of beauty breaking out on their every limb of essence.

Like us, children are bound by this law of interconnectedness. Their flawed perception of complete separation stokes their suffering. Apartness brings an ache, even as they conceive apartness from those who carry toxicity. They may be thankful and relieved to be away from such people. But a deeper place exists within youth that grieves the loss of even those people. Children walk this world asking that it love and embrace them completely. This is why they fear the world: because it might reject them.

They do not fear what they do not need. Because they need, they fear. They need all of life. So they fear all of life. This is the emotional consequence of not recognizing their togetherness. They are bound and this does not change, not even when they have conflict or grow to dislike other living things. Instructions for a close dance were sewn into children's fabric of being. Even when they grow tired of the dance or of the dance partner, the instructions remain.

When children try to pull away from the world, they suffer. When they act to deny this bond, this interflowing, they suffocate. They drown in their absence from self. For this world *is* their self. Each person, plant, thought, dream; each yesterday, now, tomorrow; every then and when; all colors of light's astounding prism; all of this is their self.

Children often feel and say to themselves: *I need to be apart from the things that wound me; that grieve me; that poison me.* But this speaks of a need for insulation, for transformation of the relationship. Not of true breaking away. There can be no absolute separation. Young people may not be able to stand this truth, but it is the backdrop to every moment. Youth are practiced at apparent escaping, but there is no actual escape.

Here is a liberating recognition children, and we, can recite: *There is no where I can go, no where I can hide, nothing I can hide behind, no distance great enough, no time long enough, to finally cleave me from those people and things I hate or fear. My being will forever affect their being and theirs will always leave a print inside mine.*

As long as I hate or fear them I am pouring poison into the well from which I drink; I am seeding my harvest ground with killing salt and making my fields of life infertile. I am breathing contagion into a closed bubble and all who breathe it become my hate and fear. Now I am surrounded by hateful, fearful people everywhere I go. I suffer from their illness but I also helped to create it. I was a contributor to this most awful stew.

We cannot overstate the importance of children recognizing their permanent joining with all things. If they do not recognize it in time, they try and slay that which threatens them. Their connection to all things cannot be slain. With every surge toward killing their offenders, they kill themselves. Every time they demean others, they spit foulness into their own chest.

Life is not a garbage dump into which youth can deposit their trash and escape its fumes. Life is both a garbage dump and a flower garden. But whatever youth scatter transforms into a more pronounced version of what they left behind and travels a quick path directly back to them. It is a boomerang wind that finds them faithfully.

What they put out ricochets against the walls of their world, their existence, and eventually strikes them. They may think: *What a painful possibility. All this cannot be true.* But the most painful truth of all is what happens when they refuse this truth and go on killing the self that lives in everything. Our task is to introduce them to this truth.

We can teach children that they exist in two forms: their big self and their small self. Their small self is defined by their physical body. Their idea of individuality is rooted here. While this part of them is valuable and should be nurtured, they should also invest in their big self. This is the part of them extending beyond their physical body. It includes other people, the natural world, and all dimensions of time and space.

Their big self is their whole identity. The big self has a parallel in the notion of *no-self*, that state of awareness in which the individual is subsumed within all of existence. This is a highly aware state of being that is at once entirely selfish and selfless.

A mantra we can teach our youth, and ourselves, to repeat is simply: *Big Me, Small Me.* This can help the idea penetrate and become imbedded in children's selfhood. The mantra can be a mental trigger for them to be considerate, compassionate, and forgiving. And when their Small Me has been demeaned, they can find refuge in their always present Big Me.

THE IMPLICATIONS OF IDENTITY

Here are some of the countless implications of identity:

ESTEEM. If we see ourselves as a vital presence in the world our esteem receives a constant infusion. Perceived connectedness opens irrigation tracks into a child, constant flowing streams that water her with worthiness. This is how esteem is grown.

COPING. Stigmatized and traumatized youth can swiftly lose their composition for coping. Coping is a mysterious thing. It depends upon children believing they can endure not only crisis, but perhaps more importantly, mundane daily challenges. Some children are more prepared to withstand another beating than they are to face apologizing for their behavior, taking a test, being laughed at because of their clothes. Coping has its roots in the ability to not perceive daily ripples as crisis. This eludes many children whose lives have been riddled with crisis emerging from moments of normalcy like landmines on the path to school. Seeing themselves as capable of managing what comes is a key to their coping.

CHOICES. In the fog of a negative or insecure identity, poor choices are likely to be epidemic. Both quick and more considerate decisions depend on children trusting their instincts. That instinct is lacking when youth are not sure what they believe, what is good for them, or what is a threat. Post-trauma, everything is a threat. To deal with this many children resort to self-defeating callousness and impulsivity as a way of taking the edge off choice-making moments.

JUDGMENT. Good judgment requires clarity. Fractured, foggy identity clouds the mental sky, making it hard to clear the mind and consider things with full awareness.

DEDUCTION. Unclear identity affects deduction processes by distorting a child's idea about why things are happening around and within her. If her sense of self is not accurate, neither will be her deductions about life.

MOTIVATION. Motivation to grow, learn, heal, forgive—motivation for anything requiring effort—is a function of a child seeing herself as capable, and seeing her connected world around her as a beneficiary of her efforts. Whole identity provides reason and is a continual whisper of encouragement.

ACHIEVEMENT. Children strive to achieve based upon their vision of self in the world. They have to see themselves as achievers in order to achieve. If they foresee how their achievement impacts the world with which they are intimately connected, this also fuels success.

BONDING AND ATTACHMENT. Children tend to develop a detached relationship with those life aspects to which they see themselves as not belonging. They become what they imagine themselves to be. Wholeness breeds bonding to the whole, which feeds back into a sense of wholeness—a circular stream.

HEALING. Viewing the world as an available, plugged-in resource encourages children to open themselves up to life's healing elements. They open their mouths to receive the coolness of the rain only because they believe that when they open their mouths something good will enter. Whole identity and viewing life as a positive potential encourage children to open their vessels to external healing sources.

COMMUNICATION. Communication is in essence an attempt at conveying one's existence. These attempts are less often made if youth question their existence. Alienation, despair, and isolation create very real doubts in youth about their existence, or at least the validity of it. To encourage their self-expression, youth need to see others, including the natural world, as capable of and willing to receive what they communicate.

ATTITUDES. Constructive attitudes have their roots in positive identities. Destructive attitudes grow from negative self-regard. Whole identity leads youth to see themselves as more beautiful and capable, and others as being the same. Angry, closed, stagnated attitudes are a symptom of a fractured identity and can be transformed by transforming youths' impressions of self.

BELIEFS. Beliefs about life and the world emerge in line with the degree to which children feel those things are truly a part of them. The more youth experience the presence of life elements within them, the more they honor those elements.

BEHAVIOR. Productive, healthy behavior is built on stable emotional and cognitive ground. Whole identity creates the sensation of stability even in the midst of change, uncertainty, and challenge.

HEALTH. Health is that state of being in which energy flows freely through a child. Her innate thoughts, feelings, inspirations, and creativity move unobstructed and without distortion. Whole identity is another way of saying that all her channels are open; i.e., she is in a state of health. She is a vessel allowing all that she is out into the world and all that the world is back into her. These outflowing and inflowing rivers are equally composed of pain and joy. Health is determined by the degree of this flow, as well as by the positive nature of the flow.

EXPECTATIONS. Identity affects expectations by either distorting or making accurate youths' ideas about the rhythms and nature of life. A broader sense of life and their place in it tends to place them in synch with natural pace, ways, and dynamics. They fall into conscious harmony with reality. This stifles self-centeredness and balances expectations of others and of themselves.

LEARNING. Children's interest in learning about the world grows the more they see the world as their extension. Their interest in learning about their internal world grows the more they realize its connection to the quality of their external life and relationships. Curiosity is not simply an intellectual drive. It is a creeping vine made vigorous by children's belief in their beauty and belonging.

TEACHING. Children's belief that they have something to teach others precedes their conscious thrust toward teaching. They have to see themselves as living lives composed of useful lessons for others. They need to notice how their individual strand shimmers in the sunlight reflected off the web of life. A teaching urge is important to children because teaching and mentoring are powerful agents for self-worth and self-discovery.

EMOTIONS. Creating a personal template for balanced, centered, proportional emotions is a foundation for healthy children. Seeing themselves as meaningful pieces in a larger puzzle grants them broader perspective. This is necessary as they manage the nature and magnitude of what they feel.

REACTIONS. As with emotions, healthy reactions depend on an accurate sense of proportion and meaning. Clarity for discerning life this way comes from internal wholeness—the capacity to see oneself fully without having that view obstructed by fears, insecurities, and toxic energy. Wholeness is the best ventilation system we can help children install.

RELATIONSHIPS. The quality of a young life is a factor of the sum of its relationships. Relationships pour into a child the vital or toxic elements he then contends with. What he carries he pours into his relationships. This circular sharing is a fact of living. Wholeness flushes out harmful blocks in the flow of relationships. It balances out and diminishes the effects of unhealthy relationships by exposing a child to healthy relationships. Every child has some beautiful internal water to pour on and transform his hurtful personal weeds.

HUMILITY. Seeing and exercising their intimate place in life's fabric creates in youth an instant humility. They find it difficult to look down on others and on nature when they realize the degree to which those things infuse them with life, enrich them, *are* them. Humility is valuable because children without humility will spew out hurtful condescension and disregard everywhere they go. This is only self-defeating, of course, because it flavors the way they are then embraced socially. Many separated children deepen their separation this way.

GRATITUDE. Gratitude comes from wholeness in the same way humility does. When children see their life connections for what they are, it is difficult for them to not be grateful. Seeing how many blessings they have, even in painful seasons, they realize how easily they could lose those things. The more they recognize the constant sweet rain of life on their personal realities, the more their hearts beat with an easy gratitude.

RESPONSIBILITY. When the *them* becomes an *us*, and the *he* becomes a *me*, born is responsibility. Once young people see their own life suspended in the fragile web of life, they are enamored of the web, careful with it, protective as a measure of self-concern.

RESILIENCE. Access to places that do not hurt and people that do not harm makes children resilient. They take what they need from those people and places to soothe themselves through the storm and calm their fears. Lightning is less frightening to youth when they are sheltered within a home. Whole identity provides a much larger, storm-proof home.

TRUST. Seeing others as their extensions helps children to view others in a more compassionate, understanding way. Forgiveness, empathy, and tolerance are flames quickly extinguished in children lacking perspective and insight. Seeing the *me* in the *them* allows children more balanced judgment of how they are affected by others. Trust requires realistic notions and expectations of others. Wholeness also sharpens discernment tools by giving young people clarity. Their confidence in pinpointing potential harm relaxes their protective impulses and gives their trust the air to breathe.

TRAUMA. Wholeness lessens the impact of initial trauma, moderates the impact of trauma's aftershocks, and speeds healing from the overall distress.

HEALING CAPACITY. As with resilience and coping, healing is fueled by access to the relationships and other vital wealth of a child's life. A child who sees herself as part of everything sees everything as an available source for transforming her pain and healing her wounds. She can also focus on the areas within her that still feel good even as parts of her feel bad.

SOCIAL SKILLS. Children pay closer attention to others when they recognize the intimate connections they share with others. Looking more deeply, children notice the subtleties in the nature of those other people. This awareness improves social skills—the ability to read and respond effectively to others, and communicate with sensitive consideration. Understanding the truth of social *interbeing* (interconnectedness), children become less judgmental, less absolute, and more accepting.

SEXUAL BEHAVIOR. Unhealthy sexuality reveals unmet yearnings for acceptance, belonging, love, affirmation, value, intimacy, connection, and for being beautiful in someone's eyes. Wholeness feeds each of these needs through functional and abundant relationships. Ungrounded sexuality is no more fulfilling to youths' true needs than cotton candy is to their hunger. Its sweetness evaporates quickly after. In fact, it often leaves pangs of remorse, deepened self-disgust, and eventually more pronounced sexual impulses. Wholeness constructs a vision of self that makes sexuality more particular. This is because whole youth are already in balance and less inclined to whimsical reactions to daily life fluctuations.

PREJUDICE. A clear relationship exists between whole identity and the plague of social prejudice: Prejudice thrives on insecurity. Whole identity increases self-security. Self-security resists prejudice. Self-security also allows for the honesty needed to admit to and reduce one's own prejudice. The more of this world children claim, the less of it remains for them to scorn.

PATTERNS OF WHOLENESS

We can construct a fairly predictive portrayal of the relationship between children and their world:

Everything in life is connected. All children yearn for a meaningful sense of that connection. They wish to belong in this world.

The more youth deviate in characteristics from social standards, the more they are vulnerable to feeling a sense of disconnection or alienation.

The most holistically healthy children have a meaningful sense of connection with every aspect of their world.

The more children feel disconnected, the more they will strive to manifest a sense of connection.

Children will strive to manifest a sense of connection in relation to the role models available.

Children will strive to manifest a sense of connection in ways that seem to them most accessible.

Every communication and interaction between adults and children should serve to nurture children's sense of whole-connection and belonging.

Creative self-expression is a powerful tool with which children can create a sense of connection.

Discipline should be administered in such a way that it helps to develop children's sense of whole-connection.

Children must have opportunities to voice themselves that are validating in order to feel connected.

All children have choices *within* their struggle. No child chooses to struggle. Disconnection and alienation are at the root of every struggle.

Children must be shown regularly how they are valued and why their life circle is dependent upon them.

Defiance is likely to increase the further a child is away from social standards.

Trust building is paramount with children whose trust has been broken in their personal lives.

Creating collective responsibility in the identity of children is essential to them reaching their potential.

BENEFITS OF WHOLE IDENTITY

Our whole identity as caregivers and advocates affects our relationship with children almost endlessly. Realizing the entire world within us creates the motivation to devote ourselves to our young. We see them not as separate entities to be served but as a meaningful part of us. We become self-serving in our devotion to them.

Wholeness increases our ability to attach to children. This is an underestimated requirement in young people's attachment to us. Vesting our complete self in children's complete self exposes the relationships to a trove of resources and affiliation channels. We gain initiative to seek out those resources and to swim back and forth through those channels.

Also increased is our ability to endure the uncertainty and temporary nature of many of these relationships. We understand more clearly that a relationship endures beyond physical proximity. We are fulfilled in knowing that we are planting seeds in one another. No matter where each of us is in the world, we will spend our future enjoying the blossoming of those seeds.

Our wholeness generates healing power necessary when these temporary relationships transition. Youth we have raised or mentored are seen not as a possession we have lost but as a form of beauty that has been forever added to our treasure chest.

We also acquire the motivation to understand, respect, and appreciate aspects of children's backgrounds and heritage. We are more grounded in our own heritage. This creates a security in embracing theirs. Out of our narrowness we welcome only narrowness from children. Out of our largeness we naturally invite their largeness.

This activated-whole balance creates efficacy and competency in relating to and caring for children. The more confident and secure we are in these relationships, the more we relax and open up. This ignites compassion and communication. Our relationships flourish. Another circular success transpires. Creativity, vision, and innovation blossom from whole identity. Vital floodgates open. Our fields are irrigated, our windows opened wide.

Whole identity is an occupation with endless benefits. It is an optimal state of being. Our physical and mental health is strengthened due to diminished stress and greater life balance. Our blood pressure and other stress-related states improve. We have less conflict with children, relating to them from our more grounded state of being. Our life is more fulfilling because we have filled more areas of it with our attention.

Our professional work with children becomes more manageable and satisfying. The more we relate to youth through our wholeness, the more they heal and overcome their challenges. Our caseload lightens as a result. Our relations with colleagues improve. We are interacting with them from a healthier more secure space.

Whole identity provides an avenue for child-centered legislation—laws that derive from a true understanding of the nature and needs of children. Whole identity reveals the subtle play of heritage and culture on both child crisis and resolution. Culture is not an element to run away from as we journey forward in laws and policy. It is the primary entry point for understanding what children need. Whole identity introduces us to children's cultural reality.

Whole identities in the general population yield stronger families and communities. This leads to a break in generational cycles such as poverty, addiction, abuse, absenteeism, and abbreviated education. Our taxpayer burden is lessened, our community and society partnerships strengthened. We learn to become genuinely communal within our activated human whole.

For a child, whole identity is just as beneficial. Her ability to endure transition and dislocation increases exponentially. Whole identity creates a buffer or insulation from harmful, threatening aspects of the world. This allows time and space for healing and tempers feelings of rejection. She knows she is more than that one aspect being attacked and therefore she is greater than the attack itself.

Her whole identity is a compass within family, life, and universe. It tells her from whence she came, where she is, and the direction she is going. It also anchors her through life's many storms.

She has more flexibility of styles for drawing the essence of self-worth. She has more buckets in the water and more wells from which to drink. Her wholeness provides access to all internal and external resources. She is more forceful in discovering herself; more assertive in defining herself; more able to heal herself.

Her ability and motivation to form attachments increase. She is offering a broader palette of herself to a broader range of people. This variety engenders success. With each success her confidence grows. Her tension and defensiveness leave her. Her walls come down. This energy transformation leads others to feel better in her presence. They give her back an energy that feels better to her. This is the mutual dance of attachment, the coupling circularity of affiliation.

The more she grows the more she gathers a motivation to grow. She realizes that surrendering into her larger being feels so much better than living tense and huddled inside of only her pain, loss, or fears. Breathing deeply and letting her love flow are a revelation. The further she moves in this direction, the more powerful she becomes. We know powerful children when we encounter them. They are the ones who remind us of the sun.

VALIDATION THROUGH CONNECTION

A young lady's whole is a sky of possibility strewn with stars of potential. Those stars remain unfulfilled in their potency until the girl is able to bring them together, connect the points. When all the stars in her sky are connected and she sees how they affect each other, her sky opens up. She is fully aware and alive.

We can help her by pointing out the connections between the stars in her sky of life. How she sings at church is related to the way she writes an assignment for school. Her choice in clothes does have a common root with her choice in friends. There is purpose in each trait she holds. Each purpose has a cross-purpose with her other traits. The meanings are hers to discover and define. We can be a part of that journey with her.

We have more practice at connecting points. By sharing with her how we have discovered the purposeful links in our lives, we give her new lenses through which to view her own existence. We are offering her new ways of seeing. We are not dictating to her what parts of her life mean. There is a subtle difference between gentle suggestion and firm assertion. We can say, *Honey, look at how happy you've made your friend with the gift you gave her.* It is another thing to say, *You need to be more giving.* The two ways may carry the same objective. They may also produce entirely different sounds against her ears.

We can also help her exercise the connections of beauty and purpose in her life. Once she sees the links she may be eager to try them out, put them on. We have gathered years of insight into how to learn from an experience at work and use it to improve our home life. We are practiced at relating one life moment to the next. Her skill may not be so polished. Our storytelling and sharing go a long way in her development. Let her see us in the process of making connections and exploring links—at home, with friends, in life. She is watching. We might as well make our performance a good teacher.

A single question tells us much about how a child sees herself: *Who are you?* We can ask her this question many ways, and regularly, as we seek to understand how she sees herself. Asking her to answer this question creatively—through drawing or storytelling, for instance— provides us even more texture. One day her answer may say to us essentially: *I am all things.* Hearing this we know she has achieved a whole identity. We should celebrate and praise her! Literally we should throw a party. Few moments are more meaningful in her life than when she achieves a state of being that sets her free!

A whole identity, once achieved, can slip away under duress. This is why *I am all things* should become a mantra for achieving and maintaining that most healthy state of seeing herself. A mantra delivers habit the same way practice delivers skill: through unglamorous repetition. She can say the mantra to herself silently in any moment, as a reminder, as encouragement, and to rebalance.

NONMALIGNANT DIFFERENCE

When we are raised and socialized to think of the unfamiliar as a threat or negative, we become people who shrink in the face of opportunities to grow. What is foreign may often be a positive learning experience or possibility. As our children develop a whole identity they begin to replace ideas of *other* and *enemy* with ideas of *part of me* and *friend*. Affiliation becomes the assumption at first encounter, even before first encounter. This does not increase their risk of harm. Their instincts are an alarm announcing itself in the presence of a true threat.

As usual, balance is the main factor in this aspect of well-being. An extreme habitual reflex of shutting down and tensing up on encounter with the unfamiliar produces a closed, inert life. This is the fearful seed for prejudice, hatred, and ignorance.

We can teach our young that they will be making discoveries all their lives. Happiness, fulfillment, and vitality are built upon a habit of making discoveries. Discovery is the nature of growth. We can encourage them to associate discovery with positive consequences. This opens them up and breaks down their calcified emotional and mental barriers.

If we teach children to see differences as nonmalignant, we open their minds and hearts to life. The alternative is closed, prejudiced, shrinking souls that could have been a garden. Those who see enemies in difference never experience a single moment of true peace, for every single person they encounter is somehow different. Those who see others as an extension of themselves encounter trusted friends everywhere they go.

FRIENDSHIP

Friendship is a prism reflecting a child's beauty back to her in a way unique to each friendship. The number of her friendships is not as important as the variety of their natures. She deserves to have a thousand curtains lifted on a thousand variations of her light. No one of us can reflect her entire beauty back to her. But her entire beauty lives in the collective circle of her true beloved.

Nature too can be her friend. If we look closely into nature we will find that we walk through a world of living things that provide us an answer to every question and all our pain. The sky, sun, stars, and moon are always speaking to us. Most older cultures understood this. A clear reason exists why so many of us, when troubled, seek refuge by the oceans, lakes, and rivers or in the woods, mountains, and meadows. We seek an old, trusted friend.

Earth is not silent. It is an endless conversation. It is we who forget how to listen. Our children began life listening to nature's wisdom. So many of them now are disconnected from nature and bound up in concrete and steel zoo-like enclosures. We can reintroduce them to nature as a compassionate ear and a loving storyteller. When we feel we are not getting through to a child or that she is not getting through to us, why not introduce her to a new friend? One that understands what it means to be filled with so much painful beauty.

RAILROAD TRACKS

Railroad tracks have for ages served as a physical and psychological barrier between communities made distinctive by heritage or material wealth. Natives of such communities learn at an early age to not go on the *wrong side* of the tracks. If they live on the wrong side they know they are considered inferior, and often internalize that inferiority. Railroad tracks also exist in the minds of children. Often these barriers are a function of children's heritage, culture, and separation experience or stigma. The tracks keep them from feeling accepted in certain social groups, in nature, or even in their new families. Success, achievement, and happiness can also live on the other side of the tracks, in their minds. The tracks orient them as to where they belong and do not belong; where they are able and unable; worthy and unworthy. Life becomes a series of nightclubs they imagine will not let them in the door, much less grant them VIP status.

How aware are we of the tracks that exist within our children? We keep pushing them in the directions we desire—socially, educationally, athletically. Are we unwittingly pushing them over railroad tracks they have been conditioned to avoid? This may explain their reluctance, resistance, or languish. Being aware of these internal barriers requires communication, openness, and sensitivity. We may discover that some of their railroad tracks are well justified and need to be honored. Others may be a product of misunderstanding and can be removed with our assistance.

They will not venture where they have a right to venture or succeed where they have the ability, if they stumble upon railroad tracks along their journey. Optimally, they will discover that there are no wrong sides of the tracks. The entire world is their neighborhood.

THE POSITIVE GRAVITY OF WHOLENESS

Humanity is a peculiar constellation. Children are planetary bodies, smaller and more vulnerable than adult planetary bodies. Each life element for a child exerts a stronger gravitational pull than those same elements do for adults. This is the spectacular vulnerability of children.

These gravitational pulls are also a clue to how we may empower children toward a healthy orbit through the world. If unhealthy elements within a girl's life space pull on her, we can expect that healthy elements will exert their own gravitational force.

When we open the entire stock of channels within her, she becomes exposed to the pull of everything that is beautiful in her world. This is the positive gravity of her whole. She is a star grounded in place by a vital web. She cannot be pulled too far by negativity or pain because she is being held in her center by the goodness coming from every direction. What creates a stable child? Activation of her wholeness. Her relationship with nature, her family, her creativity, her faith—all of this holds her in place.

CREATING WHOLENESS

Developing a whole identity is a matter of practicing those thoughts, behaviors, and actions that nurture each relationship we have within the web of life. Whole identity allows us to integrate our cultural complexities into a cohesive, healthy sense of self. A whole identity quenches the thirst for belonging and beauty, and increases self-healing capacity.

A child's wholeness is a field of growth to which we have access. We can fertilize that growth by honoring her unique song. This is accomplished as we recognize her song, learn her song, and finally cherish her song.

HONORING THE CHILD'S UNIQUE SONG

Each of us is born with an essence—a distinctive nature or character. An inclination peculiar to us alone pulls us toward some things and away from others. While we commonly understand this as personality, this truth has been honored in world cultures for centuries in a more textured sense.

Many African communities have long held that each spirit born into the world carries its own unique song. This song represents the rhythm, frequency, and flavor of life that strikes the chords of the child's spirit with the greatest degree of harmony. It is her *way of being*. Her nature. Her song is her reason for having been brought into the world. She carries a package she must deliver, an insight to join into the collective awareness of her people.

When a woman in such a community becomes pregnant, a tradition occurs, varying according to the particular tribal culture. Here is a general depiction: The expecting woman gathers her female family members and friends. They venture out away from the compound, away from the children and men and the daily noise of society. Surrounded by listening trees and sitting close to Earth, the women form a circle.

They have a singular purpose in being here: to recognize the song of this new life on its way. They spend many moments in silence, so that they can hear what nature speaks to them. Back in the compound, commotion would drown out these voices.

Protected by shade clouds from the determined sun, they laugh together and tell stories. Laughing and storytelling create good vibrations that loosen clumps of dirt blocking the unseen rivers they wear like a skirt. Inspiration begins to flow.

At times they join hands, the two closest to the waiting mother cradling her affectionately like a small child. Waiting mother massages her belly. She is not just soothing her baby, she is receiving what that precious life is already voicing. This may seem like folly to us who inhabit a reality of the tangible and who often scorn what cannot be seen. But what is the nature of all things but energy? And how does energy exist but through vibration? How are we to notice and understand a vibration except by letting it dance into us?

Night emerges to greet the circle of women. Truthfully, some of them are impatient. They want the song to come so they can get back to their lives. But this ritual is sewn into the fabric of their lives. It is what their heritage has delivered them. They have the context in which to understand this ritual's value.

Some children sing louder from their mother's belly in the night. Some become brazen in the morning. Note by note, the song emerges. The song is a love song to the world: *Prepare yourselves. I am come. Beat the drum.*

The women begin to share with each other what they are intuiting about this new child. Intuition is all we have in this world. Many of us do not believe in our intuition so it becomes a rusted tool left on the floor of our despair. These women cannot imagine not believing in a gift such as this. When they intuit, they speak what they have received to each other without self-consciousness or worrying about what the others will think.

To lie about what one intuits of a child, or to cloak that intuition in the clothes of what we desire of that child—these are bad tidings. They bring harm to the child, to the family, and to the community. Because all relationships based upon a false or disguised intuition about the child wreak havoc.

It is like being sold a bag of what we are told are melon seeds when in fact the bag contains flower seeds. Then we go about happily planting our seeds, congratulating ourselves; salivating at our expected harvest. When the harvest we expect does not come, we curse the seeds. But the seeds have done nothing wrong. They were flowers all along.

Our faulty understanding of the seeds' nature is behind our disappointment and frustration. What's more, conflicted about our failed expectations for the seeds, we fail to realize that we have been blessed by flowers. Their beauty escapes us because our limited understanding demands that they be something else.

Our children are those flower seeds. In this African setting the women continue to share what is being revealed to them about the nature-song of this child. The waiting mother's intuition is given the highest authority. This is true except in cases when an elder woman present deciphers something that helps clarify the mother's understanding of her child.

The child's song unfolds: *I am a boisterous spirit; you must allow me voice and room to move and roam. I am a quiet child; you must grant me my silence. I am a teacher, please nurture my skills. I am meant to feel things deeply; I will use this for being a healer. I am small, but my vision is large; our people would do well to fall into it and drown.*

Waiting mother and the other women reach an accord on their initial understanding of this new life on its way. This recognition of song has been the first sacred step in preparing to relate to the child in a way that will create wholeness. Wholeness depends upon being seen, recognized, and understood accurately. This is why one of the most important questions between people in many of these grandparent cultures is: *Do you see me?*

The women return to the compound and gather the people around them. Again in a circle, the women announce to the community what they have learned about the song of this new life on the way. At this point, the broader community begins its responsibility for constructing the understanding necessary to honor the child. Parents initiate conversations with their children about the waiting mother, her family, and the new child. Young people question their elders about the same. This is how we begin to prepare a safe space, a greenhouse for wholeness to grow.

A child is come! Go beat the drum! The compound of children and adults, each with a conscious stake in the new life on its way, eagerly sing the child's song during the pregnancy; not only to the child but to each other. This way, when the child emerges and begins crawling, walking, running through the community, she encounters people and places that have been drenched in her essence. What a wonderful way to make her feel beautiful!

The song is the family's and community's way of saying to the child, "*We recognize and honor that this is who you are.*" The song represents values, beliefs, personality, talents, life purpose, preferences—all of who she is.

Everyone's eagerness to sing comes from a simple understanding: that for each child who suffers in life there is a community that also suffers. For each child who thrives is a people who thrive. The degree of suffering or thriving in a child is mirrored by the amount of suffering or thriving in her people. This is a law that never changes.

The new child is bathed in her own song during her gestation; she receives this nourishment just as she receives nourishment through her umbilicus. She gestates in a bath of validation, celebration, and understanding. She is sung into beauty before she draws her first breath.

At the moment of her birth, among her first sensations are the sounds of her family and community singing to her. Along with the stark contrasts of cold air and bright light outside of the womb, she is wrapped in the warm blanket of recognition: *Welcome new child! We see you. We have planted good seeds in you. You are a seed who grows in us. You are not alone in this world. We are each other. You will never be alone.* This is a good way to begin a life.

During the important landmarks of the child's life, her loving people caress her with her song. When she learns to crawl, walk, or run, there is the song. When she learns to speak, there is the song. On her birthdays, on her first day of school, she is greeted in song. When she first menstruates she is initiated by song into the deeper meaning of her transformation. She is not allowed to breed shame inside herself for becoming a woman.

The older she grows and the more she develops, the more she dictates the nature of her song and teaches it to her people. She is the best teacher that can ever be of her song. She is granted her divinely endowed right to teach the world what she has been brought here to share.

Being imperfect, the child will struggle. This is a time when her people gather around her with determination. They sing to her more forcefully than ever. They have come to return her to herself. They recognize that punishment does not cause a struggling child to recover her vision of self. Discipline does. Discipline is a hard reminder of who we are and why we are. It snaps us back to our intended path.

In collective social harmony she receives the message: *Dear child, you are forgetting yourself. You are losing your footing. The Earth beneath you does not change. The way in which you step has changed. Remember how you began. Remember why you are. Remember the truth of how you are to be.* In Nepalese culture there is a term for this. *Shanti ko Samjhana: Remembering Peace.* This refers to the peace of the womb, the peace of our natural state, and the peace of self-understanding.

Be true to yourself. This is the one and only Yurok Indian law. Imagine how powerful this manifestation must be for a people to hold it as their essential law. When we are true to ourselves, health and prosperity flow from that cup. Most personal and social despair can be traced back to individuals failing to be true to their nature and purpose. Trueness implies the child knows herself; believes in herself; understands her purpose; and has faith that being true to that purpose and to her nature will yield a bountiful life for her and the circle of life she inhabits.

The African village sings to the child to remind her of who she herself has told them she is. They sing to say: *You are not being true to yourself. All of your suffering is a polluted water springing from the source which is your self-betrayal.* They sing so she can find her way back through her blindness to the clearing of her recognition. They sing her back home.

When the woman who was once the child becomes an elder, she is crowned with her song—a harmony always evolving as she evolves. At the moment her seasons on Earth have ended and she passes into all things, oh what a glorious song comes out: *Our dear child has become all things! She joins us now in the trees and the sky, in the water and the wind. She has not left us. She is all around us. She will visit us as she wishes, to teach again. A soul learns many things when it sits at the feet of all things.* Immersed in affirming harmony, this child has lived a good life.

RECOGNIZING THE SONG

In relating to our children who have been uprooted, it is necessary that we engage ourselves in their song. First, we must recognize their song. We cannot recognize what we cannot see, hear, touch, or feel. We cannot see if our vision is blurred; cannot hear if our listening is impaired; cannot touch if our compassion is diminished; cannot feel if our heart is fearful.

Therefore, recognizing a child's song requires more than anything self-work, internal work. Work on humility, self-security, true listening, seeing with our instinct instead of our assumptions or expectations; reckoning with our prejudices; clearing out our life pollution; inviting and encouraging the child's creativity; creating a safe space for the child.

The stakes in recognizing a child's song are heavy. The discrepancy between his natural song and the tone of life around him can also be described as a cultural mismatch. It is in this sense that culture and cultural harmony are determinants of the quality and prosperity of a child's life. Some dismiss heritage and culture as things to bulldoze under with smug allegiance to what they are comfortable with. This is how we bury a child's song and thereby our opportunity for a healthy relationship with him. We bury his opportunity to grasp his own beauty and relax in knowing that he belongs. Beauty and belonging are a source and a consequence of a child singing his song.

LEARNING THE SONG

Recognizing the song is just the beginning. As a child grows, his understanding of himself increases. He tries in many ways to let us know who he is. He is trying out his song, auditioning for himself. We have to join him in this. We have to move beyond recognition and learn his song. Learning requires repetition of the song by both us and the child. We both need to practice consistently, daily. We should practice together and alone. Both kinds of practice yield their own unique benefits. When he notices us *practicing him* on our own time, this tells him that we care and are invested.

When we practice piano, violin, painting—any creative endeavor—we require a safe space. We also need to maintain safe, stable spaces in our lives where we can practice his song. He needs those safe spaces, too. And we should create opportunities to sing the song. Annual birthday songs are nice but where is his daily serenade? We can create traditions for this.

Communication between us and this child whose song we study is critical. Our communication, verbal and nonverbal, should be consistent, honest, gentle, and patient. This is what we mean by compassionate listening and loving speech—skills we must practice. Communication with a child opens up the channels through which his song can flow. It is like opening up the doors to a cathedral or opera house. Standing outside, the song comes bursting through. The symphony splashes over us. The child is playing notes and reaching crescendos we did not notice before. Open up all the doors in your house! A song is trying to come through!

CHERISHING THE SONG

We cherish a child's vital song by building opportunities to sing it into our family and community life. Societies who cherish their children's song build these same opportunities into the culture of society. We cherish by singing. Cherishing involves daily praise and celebration. We can establish traditions and rituals related to the song. Our lives can become rituals through which we sing each other's song back and forth. This is reciprocity, mutuality. It is the true nature of friendship.

Each of us moves through life passages daily. If we look closely and with an open mind, we can see that every transition is important because it is a waterfall in a river of waterfalls. By singing children's songs to them as they pass over these daily and seasonal waterfalls, we smooth their ride downriver to the ocean of their becoming. Rivers have hard rocks in them. Cherishing smoothes those rocks. Cherishing is an act that polishes the way.

We can also cherish a child's song by promoting and publishing it. There are many ways to do this. When we frame a child's artwork on the living room wall, we have both promoted and published the work. It is a matter of our creativity. We have the ability to think of ways to let others know about a child's song.

We also cherish by teaching the song to others. The more a child's teachers, friends, coaches, and neighborhood are familiar with her song, the more she realizes how much we cherish her. She knows we are the ones who are putting the tune out there.

We can not overestimate the value of complimenting her on her song. This world is a battering tide that does not relent in eroding her sense of beauty. It does not cease making her doubt her purpose or the value of her desires.

When we cherish her as a matter of daily breathing, we build fortresses to protect her against that swallowing tide.

In that culture is our way of being, we recognize that her song is in fact her personal culture, her unique *way*. Her quest to have her song heard, understood, and sung back to her is in fact a quest for cultural integrity.

The venerable Vietnamese Buddhist monk Thich Nhat Hanh has written: *True love needs understanding. With understanding the one we love will certainly flower.* The Teacher is calling us to move beyond adoration. He is saying our children need us to end our love affair with surface embraces. They need us to do the hard work that leads us deep into their truth. They need our understanding. The moment we reach that place, we are showering them in affirmation and belonging. Our understanding is their sunlight, water, and Earth. They have been waiting so long for this divine spring season. Now they let down their guard. Now they flower. Love *and* honor. We have this power.

CULTURAL BLINDNESS

Cultural blindness causes us to not see each other. It exists when we experience others through the perspective of our own culture, dismissing the relevance of their culture. Commonly, cultural blindness afflicts those in mainstreams as they relate to those in the side streams. Being in a side stream usually forces us to become competent in the mainstream culture; we become bicultural. Cultural blindness is therefore often a one-sided affliction in a relationship.

Our blindness leads us to judge people out of context. We have placed them in a context: that of our culture.

Until we make an effort to place them in the context of the heritage and culture that shapes them, we relate to them in damaging ways.

Miscommunication is one of the symptoms of cultural blindness. Cultural differences between adults and children create a minefield of miscommunication waiting to happen. Miscommunication may seem like an innocuous thing, but it can lead to unnecessary labeling, conflict, violence, and even death.

Within families, such miscommunication halts bonding and introduces alienation. In the relationship between children and institutions, this kind of miscommunication leads to youth being inappropriately tracked scholastically. It also leads to culturally disparate case assessment, decision-making, treatment, planning, and resolution.

Cultural blindness causes failures to identify a child's strengths. His misunderstood nature goes unappreciated. Everyone, including him, misses out on his valid gifts and forms of beauty. Opportunities for his healing and growth are bypassed. Not seeing his strengths leads to a plague of cognitive, emotional, and behavioral misdiagnoses.

How can any approach be truly strength-based if it is not grounded in consideration of his cultural reality? Many of his strengths come to life inside of that reality. Bacteria do not grow in the wrong medical culture. There is a reason that a Petri dish and its contents are called a *culture*: things grow best in the environments that feed their true nature. Child strengths do not fully materialize or reveal themselves through a foreign cultural perspective. Approaches to children that call themselves strength-based are only engaging in rhetoric until they humble themselves to learning a child's true *ways of being*.

Cultural blindness also results in misidentification of a youth's weaknesses and challenges. Our inability to truly see him can cause us to incorrectly determine his intent, motivation, behavior, fault, capacity for rehabilitation, and so forth. He is at the mercy of blind people who are certain we spot his flaws when in fact he is trying to flag us down. There is an obstruction on the road he walks. He only wants us to notice.

Perhaps most destructive of all, cultural blindness creates a second blindness. So convinced are we of our good intentions that we fail to notice our bad impact on his life. Our condescending-charity attitude in the way we look at him is the unfortunate consequence of our savior mentality. We resist any suggestion that questions our expertise and authority. We are offended at the slightest mention of a possible cultural misunderstanding. After all, *all children are the same*, are they not? Our defensive attitude and the way we fail to see him are ripe for resulting in destructive laws, policies, practices, and services. Our embrace of him has thorns.

CONDESCENDING CHARITY

Out of the cage of imposed eternal gratitude a deafening silence emerges. The absence of a child's voice should be an alarm to our sensibilities. We have muzzled her with a startling message that serves at once as label and warning: *You are a child for whom many selfless things have been done. You have been taken in, sacrificed for, endured. For all of this we expect that you heal, trust, bond, smile, open up, calm down, straighten up, back down, pick up, slow down, join us, become us, leave your shameful past and parts behind. And we expect this of you as soon as you can possibly manage. After all, our tolerance has its bounds.*

Charity, in its original spiritual sense, is an act of the mind and heart that enriches our spirit by virtue of compassion. Compassion requires not sympathy but empathy: understanding. Understanding requires respect: our doorway into another person's true self. True charity is the ultimate, beautiful, self-serving act. Through charity we serve self in a most honorable way: by recognizing the presence of self in others. With this recognition we are motivated to beautify the human tapestry.

Too often, and well-meaning, we think of ourselves as performing a selfless act by *helping out* a child in need. This easily solidifies into an attitude of condescending charity. Our helper's identity becomes one of having sacrificed on behalf of the child, who should now be forever grateful. This is one of the most destructive attitudes to which youth are exposed. Condescending charity crushes esteem, attachment, and voice. It creates anger and resentment. Condescension consistently defeats good intent.

Being involved with dislocated children is not selfless but fulfilling to the self. We are not *helping out* or *lifting up* a child. We are *serving* or *raising* a child. Not only do we embrace her, she embraces us. Whatever form of relationship we have with her, she is giving us the same things we give her. We need only look closely to see this.

In our relationship she is not only the student but the teacher; not only the mentored but the mentor. She should no more be grateful for what we have done for her than we should be for what she has done for us.

A child who feels pain and a need to express it should feel empowered to do so, without having to fear being criticized or punished for being ungrateful. We freely express our frustrations to her and around her. Muting her voice is not only contradictory, it damages our relationship. These children are not burdens in our life. They are blessings:

How messy an affair is child well fare
how wicked the brew that failed families do
how pitiable the child thrown to the wild
so in ride the saviors
their chariots afire
to bend down and scoop up
the tragic children who forevermore
shall be in their debt

foul charity has been done
the moon is unstrung
and free to conduct the dance of the tides
but wait
who here in this unkempt equation is saved
and who is the salvation?

Here is the hint . . .
God's grace is granted in golden gifts
the gifts are untidy because a child wrapped them.

A MAN AND A BABY SNAKE

A man came upon a baby snake struggling alongside the road on a hot day. Feeling compassion for the baby snake the man carefully picked it up and took it home. He placed the baby snake in a nice aquarium, filled it with pretty stones, and included a bowl of fresh drinking water. He went to the library and studied up on the diet of snakes, then provided food to the snake on a regular basis. He positioned a lamp nearby for heat. Then he sat back and waited, expecting the snake to recover and thrive.

The baby snake continued to languish and grow weaker. The man grew increasingly frustrated, saying to the baby snake: *I don't understand why you are not thriving and happy. I have done all these things for you. I took you out of*

the withering heat and brought you into my cool home. I have
given you all the things I assume a snake like you would need.

The baby snake, being a snake and, therefore, not capable of speaking in a human tongue, remained silent and listless. One night the man was visited in his dreams by the baby snake. The man took the opportunity to confront the snake. He demanded: "Will you finally answer me as to why you have not responded to my loving care according to my expectations?"

The baby snake, this being a dream, responded in the man's tongue: "I was in fact struggling by the side of the road that day you came and took me to your home. And yes, it felt good to be out of the heat. I also was grateful for your kindness. But although I was struggling when you found me, at least I was struggling in my own environment. At least there were other snakes struggling alongside me who could relate to my experience.

"Since being in your loving care my struggle has worsened. Now my initial wounds have deepened because I have been given absolute aloneness along with the burden of your expectations. I have felt you expecting me to get better. You have been so kind to me that I did not want to disappoint you, and so I have tried hard to transform myself as you desire. The problem is that you never found a way to look deeply into me and understand who I am. I am not your vision of a snake. I am a snake. I have my own actual truth that escapes your insight. My suffering therefore also escapes your insight.

"It is not that you have no chance of helping me but you cannot help me if our relationship is led by your own reality alone, by your own way of seeing and being. You assumed my struggle was the heat, so you took me from the heat. You never took me from my true struggle—it still lives within me. And now I also have your struggles with assumption, bias, and frustration to manage."

The man, hearing all of this, was taken aback. Grappling with his understanding, he asked the baby snake, "Please tell me, how can I help you?"

The baby snake, relieved, responded, "By allowing and encouraging me to be the snake that I am, not the snake that you imagine me to be. The path to my healing lies there."

The man's dream ended then. He awoke in a warm sweat of realization. The next morning he took the snake to a cool meadow near a stream. They began that day to have silent conversations with each other about the nature of things. The man visited the baby snake regularly and learned many new things about the snake and about life. By the time the baby snake had grown into maturity the man too had left behind his baby-state and discovered himself. His true state was as a brother to all living things and a lover of life's essential variety.

COLORBLIND ABANDONMENT

Leaving children alone to face the persistent rain of prejudice—the steady erosion caused by always being *the other*—is its own form of abandonment. It is a virulent form of neglect. An insidious fade occurs with a child abandoned into otherness. Her integrity fails. She literally begins to break into pieces in places hidden so well we do not notice.

We might say that physical abandonment is worse. But do we know this? The young girl might say, "At least with physical abandonment everybody knows I have been left alone. With this blindness, you preach about how I am no different from you. Everyone thinks I am so richly loved. When I express otherwise I am the girl who cried wolf. I am called ungrateful. I'd rather be abandoned in a way that people notice than to be left alone inside a secret only I possess."

As parents and advocates, we feel that we embrace children and give them shelter from the turbulence. But there is a hole in our roof. The tear was created by our negligence. Our youth keep getting drenched in social infamy. We refuse to dry them off because of our commitment to not focusing on the social elements that drench them. All of this is in the name of sameness. This is how to raise a confused child.

If we mean to tell children that prejudice is wrong, then we should communicate this clearly. Lazily casting terms like *colorblind* at them can create reckless and unintended impact. If we seek to teach them to not judge people and to appreciate uniqueness, then we should simply say so. Avoiding the realities of human prejudice is a poor substitute for teaching a direct social lesson.

We often simplify and make benign our messages to youth about their life experiences. We do this by interpreting their lives to them, outside of the historical context that is generating those experiences. This bleaches and dilutes the insight we offer youth for their piercing emotions and thoughts. They need more honesty from us.

We believe that if we close our eyes and wish hard enough all the difficult substance of their heritage and life story will go away. It is time to open our eyes. We are missing out on our children. Even worse, we risk not noticing their fade from life. Colorblindness often leads to a colored death.

A reflexive, epidemic claim of many parents is: *I love and treat all my children the same.* This is a good epidemic to avoid! This may be our attempt to prove that we love our children the same *amount.* Our message can be interpreted by children very differently: as a sign that we devalue what makes them unique. This can make them feel loved less, not more.

Sameness of treatment does not erase a child's heritage, separation trauma, or her feeling that she is an outcast in the family or community. Homogenous treatment only prevents us from dealing responsively with her unique needs.

A whole child is standing before us waving her hands frantically as if to say, "Can you see me?" We believe we can get away with ignoring parts of her that discomfort us, parts that we feel are triggers for her suffering. Ironically, our avoidance triggers her suffering. Let us please stop trying to not see parts of the child. Instead, let us try to see those parts in a more beautiful way.

On the beach, two boys play by the tidal foam. With cracked plastic buckets they gather wet sand and build castles. One boy asks the other: *Why don't you look like your parents?*

The other boy looks back over his shoulder at his parents, sunning themselves on blankets. He answers: *In our family we're colorblind.*

What does that mean?

The answer comes out rapid-fire, rehearsed, a mantra meant to comfort even though it seems to cause him pain: *We don't see color. We don't care about color. All colors are beautiful.*

How can all colors be beautiful if you can't see them?

The boy from the colorblind family is not used to speaking about these things. He is used to keeping his feelings to himself about being a different color from his family. Even at home where he is not supposed to have any feelings about color at all.

The other boy is perplexed. With a caring heart he offers: *Maybe you all can go to the doctor and she can fix your*

*family so you won't be blind anymore. Then your dad would
notice that his skin is red and burning in the sun!*

Life could never be colorblind
she is a fool in love with color
she has become so enamored
she is flushing tipsy
she inflates Earth with
gusts of lavender, scarlet, sable
till it is a paint balloon
perched on edge of table
about to burst

boom!

life is laughing her deepest laugh
she has kicked Earth balloon over
spraying valleys emerald
mountain passes glacier white
oceans take on hue of ecstasy

she is a child giddy chasing
the mad décor of her Creation kite

variety swims in her eyes
she can't see straight
she misses the lines
could not care less
fiends for this dancing light

this mess is what she is living for
she kicks blue across the cypress floor
coral red jumps from sea and joins the spill
blue becomes purple dusk unreal

she is rolling in leaves
of every tone
she isn't done yet
she gathers every color
and paints her throne

color is not a coating
it is the dripping of the root

with each chanting of
we don't do color in our house
the devotee of these words grows
more self-satisfied while the child
done in color perishes

you may say *we don't do color*
but life does color
it does it beautifully
if we should draw a hint from anything
it should be from Life

do color
do it beautifully
color is the doorway
into the archives of a soul

color is the flag bearer
for a parade of human testimony

color is why the Artist painted
in the first place
painted this child this way
for this reason

for Goodness sake
do color.

HERITAGE IS MORE THAN COLOR

Color on its own is beautifully meaningful. Color is more than pigment. It is an indication of the collective journey preceding us. That still unfolds within us. Color should not be a trigger for our assumptions. This does not mean that color is meaningless. Or that color is the sum of our heritage. It is a hint of our generational journey.

Even so, reducing a child's heritage down to a color is an incredible insult. Doing so allows us to believe that her heritage is meaningless. Her heritage is much greater than just her color. Entire generations lived, loved, suffered, and accumulated wisdom in the folds of her heritage. To call all of that her color is just our way of giving ourselves permission to wash her heritage down the sink.

Here is a gift we give children by telling them: Do not ever allow someone, anyone, to reduce your heritage to a color. Legions of ancestors died and carried crying hearts to smooth your path. Everything beautiful poured itself into you through the generations of your heritage. When people reduce your heritage to a color, this insult is the beginning of them erasing you. Once you are a color they can say that color is meaningless.

People love to dismiss color even as they have spent their whole lives choosing to be surrounded by their own color. They especially love to say this when their color controls the definition of beauty. Control the definition of beauty and you control your world, large or small. You have been blessed with an inheritance that no one can steal from you. If it were not so priceless the thieves would not be so relentless or so many.

Many of us believe that the older a child is when we become a part of his life, the less we have to worry about his heritage and culture. We assume this because we feel he has already acquired or developed his cultural personality and identity by the time of our acquaintance.

This season of his life finds him perhaps confused more than ever about his place in the world. He tries on new cultural clothes every day. He may seem almost foolish in his wild swings and assertive stands. He is feeling himself out. This is his journey. He needs us to not ridicule or demean his presentation.

Two seasons are wrestling in his mind: the boy with the man. He has a very good idea what we wish him to be culturally. Whatever we may say, our true feelings betray us in every moment. What eludes him is his own clarity and security about what he wishes to be. He is beginning to build the house of notions that he will inhabit across his many moons.

Another common mentality is that the younger a child is when she comes to us the less we need to address her heritage. Underlying this attitude is the misconception that her heritage is nothing more than the product of socialization. Since she has been removed from her past environment we believe her heritage will somehow magically dissolve into ours. We even convince ourselves that she may not have developed her culture yet, rendering her lineage obsolete. This notion is entirely false. Her individual and collective pasts live so potently within her that there is no expiration date.

Some of us dismiss ideas about certain social groups of children by saying: *That is true of all children.* We should be careful to not let smugness cause us to bypass an opportunity to gain insight. When we discuss groups we are discussing degrees, intensities, patterns, trends, streams. We are not reducing individuals into categories.

But neither should we assume that because all children share certain truths that no child experiences her own singular truth. Our human truths are both unique *and* common. This is inescapable. Uniqueness and commonality are not mutually exclusive. Our challenge is to move beyond lazy thought into the realm of true reflection. When we do, we are more than capable of understanding this of a child: She can at the same time be a part of a collective truth and her own unique truth.

A vital reason why we would honor a child's heritage is because it is her story. If we do not take her story seriously, we are likely to overlook the fact that she is a unique individual. Once we do that we become the blind, insensitive force whose presence in her life creates injury.

If when we think of the word *heritage* we imagine a group of people, all sharing the same ways of being, we are imagining an unproductive idea. Heritage flows into us throughout life from an accumulation of individuals. We filter, process, and manifest that heritage in unique individual ways.

Honoring a girl's heritage is just the opposite of generalizing her into a group. It is a doorway into her individuality. Inside that room she teaches us the meaning she has made of her heritage. That lesson is her culture, a forever transforming, flowering statement to the world.

CHANGING HER NAME

Many old cultures of the world take a child's name so seriously that great care and time is taken in naming the child. Ceremonies developed over ages spiritually enact the naming of this new life. Her spirit has a purpose. Therefore it has been equipped with a nature. Her name honors her purpose and nature. It honors her people and generations. It honors an entire human experience. She has been given her name by her people. It is a permanent umbilical cord between her and her origin.

And yet so many families grasp a child out of her heritage and culture and immediately strip her of her familiar name(s). When we do this, our reasons are always the same: *We want to make it easier on her as she grows up and in her career.* The truth is we want to make it easier on us. We want to give her a name and in doing so seal our possession of her. We want a name that we like and are familiar with. We want her to fit in better with her new siblings. We want, we want, we want. When does what we want defer to who she is?

Our reasons for renaming her may be understandable, but is our action honorable? Separation has already taken her from her roots. Now we have pulled her root, by virtue of her name, from the soil of her being. For those who come from a slavery heritage, this is more than vaguely reminiscent of the auction block. The shearing of names reminds indigenous people the world over of the shearing of their children's sacred locks in boarding schools. It has the scent of *the civilization of savages.* This is one reason that so many witness the movement of children across this Earth and cry out *Genocide.*

In and of itself, giving a child a name, out of our love, is a beautiful thing. But why not give her an additional name rather than replacing her nominal connection to her source? A child cannot have too many names given in love. They do not all have to be part of her legal name. In many cultures children carry six and seven names. Can we stretch our imagination beyond our cultural constraints and endow her with more than first, middle, and last?

Some of us are possessive about naming a child. We even resent the ideas that her other parent and relatives suggest to us. But they are not just suggesting. They are expressing their heart's inspiration. The name that comes to them is their vision of her. Why do we have to be so possessive with her name? She does not belong exclusively to us. We get to be her nearest chaperone. The whole world cares that she comes home safely.

THE ILLUSION OF THE INDIVIDUAL

When we step onto an elevator with another individual, we are not the only two people in that space. Our bodies create illusions of separateness that deceive us and lead us down harmful roads. On that elevator we share a space not only with that other person but also with everyone who is or who has been a part of her life. We are encountering her ancestors, relatives, family, and community. We are meeting her pain, joy, fears, assumptions, prejudice, love, compassion, and life experiences.

All of this exists within the person as potentials. At any instant, something about us, the elevator, and the moment may interact to awaken one or more of her potentials. This awakening is the cause of how that person treats us in that closed space of the elevator.

The child in the elevator with us is an entire people. Her scowl and avoidance of eye contact are hand-me-down clothes that have been passed to her by someone else. Even her smile is second-hand clothing she picked up along the way from someone who wore it as a mask to hide sadness.

The same is true of what we bring into the elevator with us. We bring all the people of our life, all of our experiences, all of our sensitivities. When two people encounter each other on an elevator, two worlds of people and experiences are coming together. There may be silence in the elevator, but the silence is loud. This is background conversation is what shapes relationships.

Many people continue to struggle with grasping this essential truth about the relational web of human nature. Perhaps this resistance is the cultural artifact of societies that, for better or worse, are so engrained with notions of individuality, separation, and fragmentation—within people and between people and the world.

When a child comes into our life, two worlds are coming together, not two individuals. This is the importance of considering, examining, and honoring heritage and culture. Both concepts are simply another way of describing the totality of who a person is.

Viewed in this light, it becomes easier for us to understand that it is not possible to separate a child from her culture or heritage. A child *is* her culture and heritage. No part of her exists outside of or independent of these things. Her spirit, essence, and personality are so intimately interwoven with her heritage (life inheritance) and culture (way of being) that to attempt to perform a surgery to separate these elements would kill the patient.

Sometimes we resent or are angry toward people who are a part of a child's past. Our drive to close those people out of a child's present and future is then built upon spite and self-interest. This is a shame because it overshadows and poisons the impact of the appropriate concerns we have about people from her past. Our personal emotions toward a child's roots do nothing to change what those roots mean to her fundamentally.

Even if she is hateful toward her kin she needs for us to speak well of them. If we attack her source, we attack her. If we demean her people, we shred the cord between her and us. Her heartstrings bind her to her roots and extend outward toward us. It is a single strand. Whichever segment we cut unravels the full length of her being.

She may adopt our resentful, negative attitudes toward her roots. But that season often ends. Something rises in her, an undeniable force. Roots exert a relentless gravitational pull. When she realizes that she has been taught a distorted view of her roots by those she depended on for her well-being, relationships are damaged. New anger and resentment emerge in a child who has already had to deal with the wounds of her past.

Maybe her original family members are superstars in her eyes. They may have been the most wonderful family a child could ask for. Now we feel we are competing with legend. That is our problem: This is not a competition. It is a relay trek. Her family has passed the child-baton to us. The baton has a tender heart, fantastical vision, and a destination. Teachers, mentors, guardians—all of us carrying a golden baton toward her divine potential.

Yes, she is her own unique individual. This does not mean that she is a floating object void of any meaningful relationship with the world she comes from. There are things in her. Those things are her stuff. She sees herself in us when we acknowledge her stuff. When we take good care of her stuff.

Who are we to burn, shred, or discard the material of a child's past? We are burning, shredding, discarding the child herself. These things are her access to herself; they may one day hold the key to her healing. This material and information are not our possession. They are hers. She must be given the opportunity to discard what she wishes, when she is in a healthy place of self-determination, at whatever age that may be.

She may choose to embrace what we wish or assume she would throw away. Her scrapbook of pain is not separate from her scrapbook of joy. They are the same book. As she grows she will discern how to edit that book, how to decorate it, how to know herself through it, who to share it with. In her whole life there is no book that will ever be more her rightful possession. No one else may choose to destroy her treasure chest.

A child comes from somewhere. Comes from something. Comes from someone. We cannot assume what this means. We assume that it means something. There, we have honored her truth.

Her heart journal reads: *I hear whispers from far and aching shores. It is my great and distant Ama. She whispers to light a fire and keep me warm.*

CHILD AMBASSADORS

A child's soul is a pristine bowl filled with her essence. With each strike of disrespect to her cultural heritage we pierce that bowl. We puncture its protective sheath, opening up holes. The child's soul becomes a colander, a bowl blemished with openings, no longer water tight. This is how her essence leaves her: through the holes that we have made in the pouch of her heritage.

Every child is an ambassador representing each aspect of the cultural complexity within her. The fundamental question we must ask when considering and intervening in her life is: *What country (whole life reality) do you come from?* The more familiar we are with her interior landscape the less damage we do. Walking in the dark through a child's interior, we stumble over her corners and trample her valued belongings.

What country do you come from? This is not a literal question. It is a function of our culture-honoring relationship with her. We must ask this question in such a way that she feels safe to reveal her country. Then we must develop a relationship with that country. We are not done yet. We need to also ask ourselves the same question: *What country do I come from?* Our own ambassadorship entirely affects our relations with hers.

FEAST DAY

Note: This segment represents a poetic personal interpretation of the public aspect of a sacred ceremony into which the author was several times invited. It is not intended as an authoritative statement on a people's cultural reality.

Along the Rio Grande River corridor of northern New Mexico, communities of people live who have inhabited the land for a great many seasons. They are the Pueblo people. *Pueblo* being the Spanish word for town, these Native people live in modest communities, mostly along the river in the high mountain desert.

Each of these 19 pueblos has a distinct culture within the larger Pueblo culture. Each community also has its own annual day(s) during which dancing, prayers, and communal feasting take place. These are called feast days.

On these grand days, inside family homes, great meals are served on the long table. The meals are for the family, family friends, the entire community, and for visitors from outside the pueblo. Wave after wave of people comes into the home, waits respectfully until someone has left

the fully occupied dining table, and then joins the meal.
This is how a people come together. Conversation flows as
easily as the sweet wild tea. Generations pass the muster
of intimacy with each other.

People come to know each other in new ways.
Photographs tell stories on the walls. *Stranger* is a strange
concept for this extended family within the pueblo. A
symbolic opening occurs as family after family opens its
home to its people. Family and community are speaking to
one another, saying: *You are welcome here. You are one of us.*

The dining tables are filled over and again with food:
piles of Pueblo bread, fry bread, and tortillas; thick,
glistening stacks of corn; and deep bowls of chilé, pasolé,
and frijoles. Diners are urged on persistently by the
servers: *Eat plenty. Eat plenty.* Diners' stomachs bursting,
they politely excuse themselves on over to the next home
and the next meal.

More giving takes place during another, important kind of
feast day, one celebrated by some of the pueblos. During
these feast days, a wonderful act occurs on the rooftops.
Families have gathered as much food, drink, and other
goods as they can. They have brought it up to the roof of
the home and prepared for the mass arrival. The
community, in hundreds, comes pouring down the dirt
roads, engulfing family homes as they flow. Entire
families, gathered on their rooftops, joyfully begin
throwing grocery items, Pueblo bread and other baked
goods down to the crowd below. Children are often at the
forefront of this giving task. They are being taught.

It is hard to tell whether the families are more joyful
in giving or the people below are more pleased by their
receiving. The message is clear: Families are giving back to
the community from which they have received so much—
support, protection, togetherness. The community is

receiving from the families. In the loud cheering of the throngs a message is delivered to the rooftop families: *We are happy to receive your offering. In doing so, we recognize your beauty and richness among us.*

This vibrant, generous transaction between family and community involves many people who have relatively little. And yet they are giving so much: so much love, openness, and possession; so much more than what is given outside the pueblo land in places with more tangible wealth to give.

There is a saying: *Give what you got.* These people understand: Mutuality and reciprocity are the most beautiful *selfish* acts to which we can devote ourselves. The acts are communally selfish in that they benefit the self through service to others. Reciprocity creates our well-being. In these Pueblo homes, on these Pueblo rooftops, the web of life is a finely tuned string instrument being played for all its worth.

Here, in our own lives, when we receive children who have come from elsewhere, and else other, we have a glorious opportunity. We can honor the spirit of the many people, places, and experiences that actively pulse inside the youth. In doing so, we are giving back to the source from which we have received the children. This strengthens our relationship with the youth, makes them whole. The whole child becomes our gift back to that source. The whole child, in the way she goes on to live her life, somehow strengthens and heals her original community, the people of her heritage. She is empowered to empower her source. This is how we honor the community of origin.

A further challenge beckons us: Why not invest ourselves in caring more about these source families and communities? The way in which we live often passively contributes to their continued suffering and material poverty. Our non-caring contributes to the continued social inequities between us. Are we large enough to directly engage these people as humble sisters and brothers, to learn from them, and explore how we can enrich one another? Reducing our prejudice and callousness toward them alone creates positive change.

We can adopt a helpful mantra in this regard. We can tell ourselves repeatedly: *Give what you got.* This will remind us of the Pueblo families giving away their food and water, and opening up their homes and hearts. It will remind us that we never just help an individual child. Each time we do so we are entering a pact of mutuality with the generations of good souls who live inside the child.

Possessing children with ruptured roots should not be the goal of a compassionate society. We proudly proclaim our love and care for these children. Our individual heart should not let us rest until we love and care for the people these children come from. This compassion becomes the collective action that heals and strengthens the source. We should care this much: that the children we claim to love stop flooding out of the arms of their first embrace. We should want them to not ever need our rescue.

In the pueblo center, on feast days, an awesome celebration takes place. Adorned in traditional dress, male and female, young and elderly Puebloans pound the dry earth in cadence to the pounding drum. In fluid, moving lines and circles, beneath the beating sun, the dancers sing their remembrance and worship of the Great Spirit, their Pueblo people, their generations, their blessings.

The drumbeat and dancer movement are hypnotic. All that these people have ever been and ever will be comes pouring into the moment. The dancers' voices emerge from a core place inside. Their movement is proud, powerful. It is as if with each dancer step, each touching of a foot upon the Earth, a pact is reenacted:

We must take good care of the children
We must take good care of their first family
We must take good care of their first community
We must take good care of their ancestors
We must take good care of ourselves
All of this will take good care of us
This is the circle of life
It feeds us well
Let us eat plenty
Eat plenty.

ROOTS

A child is a tree. Her roots weave through the Earth. That those roots may not be visible to us does not mean they are nonexistent. Every healthy child necessarily has viable roots. What tree has ever thrived without its roots? There are plants capable of regrowing their roots, but the roots they regrow are of the same nature as the original ones. This is the pulsing, never-ceasing determination of a living thing to stabilize itself through its roots. Those roots provide access to water that is the nutrition of living. The water comes from the Earth, which for a child is her social ground.

If you could have all the painful experiences of your life wiped from your memory and extracted from your heart, would you? What if to achieve this you would also have to endure the deletion of all your positive experiences and those you love? Everyone and everything you care about would be gone, your memory wiped clean of their existence. How do you feel imagining this extreme vacating of your life's heritage?

Incredibly, this is what many of us as caregivers, and advocates consider doing or actually do to children. We feel it is in their best interest to protect them from their hurtful past or from those who hurt them. But we cannot cut out hurtful parts of a child's life without also cutting out the beautiful parts, the essential parts of who she is.

This does not mean that we need to carefully preserve and keep present her hurtful environments, situations, and people. It means that, like us, she deserves, needs, and has a human right to access the entire bounty of her life. It is not our place to determine what she is allowed to carry forward. We cannot project what aspects of her pain she might transform into her beauty. In trying to take her pain from her, we often and unwittingly also steal from her some of the resource for her healing and wholeness.

A child's roots do not ever truly disappear. She just experiences seasons during which she does not feel or recognize those roots. Our presence either makes her roots more visible and alive or it buries them further. We may be pleased to see her live as though she is rootless. That way she can become our image. As long as she feels rootless she feels as though she is floating. A floating child will never settle in our arms. What means more to us: that she imitates us or that she truly becomes a part of us?

A rainbow crests the sky joining a child to her ancestors. This rainbow supersedes any wrong her immediate family may have done. She may be in our hands now but she belongs to the ages. She is a generational force forging ahead to create a new day. It is not our place to disrupt this ancient flow. No excuse exists for us to cancel out her past and the people who populate it.

If we cannot summon the slightest respect or notion of goodness for her broader people, we face a reckoning. Our disdain for her roots, or our insecure need to possess her exclusively, is sure to cause her great harm. Our resentment will only grow for the spirits of those who live within her. Unable to separate her spirit from theirs, she is our resentment's destination. If we cannot cure our hearts in this regard and will ourselves to honor her heritage, we might easily become her greatest current abuser. Our abusive fist will be a drove of repudiations.

She has the right to conceive her family tree in ways that encompass all who have touched her life. Focusing on kinship rather than legal guardianship allows integrity to her tree, rather than splinters, fractions, and fragments.

Her heart journal:

I will not transcend my roots
you need to transcend your fear of me
transcend your fear of me
your fear of me
fear of me
of me
me.

FORCED CHOICE OF LOYALTIES

He is torn between pleasing his roots, which are a voice just as loud and present as any other, and pleasing those of us in his current life. This tension is largely created by our dichotomous relationship with his past. Our threatened hearts seek closure and resolution. Another way of saying this is that our hands are full of nails and hammers, desperate to permanently close the door on his past. We have allowed ourselves only a rigid, either-or proposition: We allow his past and suffer or we snuff it out. By extension these are the only options we allow to him.

Our message reaches him in subtle and surprising ways: *Love us and be one of us, or love them and betray us and what we have done for you.* We have forced him into a dichotomy of loyalties. How unfair. How impossible. A child and his social inheritance: These two things, more so than any nation or manmade thing, are indivisible.

A myth exists that says the communities from which many of these children come don't care about taking care of their young in crisis. This is offered as the reason for taking children out of their communities. These communities do care. They are averse to mainstream ways of handling youth in crisis; especially those from side streams: possession, ownership, separation. In the eyes of these origin communities, such mainstream ways are unnatural, unhealthy, and lacking in humanism.

Replacing family, heritage, and culture is unnecessary and suspect. There is no child crisis that cannot be addressed by expanding rather than replacing a child's source. Expanding a child's family and community diminishes the identity fractioning that results from legal and social notions of replacement. Expansion lessens the pressure on children to choose sides and loyalties. They have no partitioned family or reality for which they must cleave their hearts. They are allowed to remain in possession of a *whole* family, community, reality. Physical separation does not disallow this inclusive embrace.

There is an aspect of their journey that is not ours. Our quality as expanded family is not defined by the meaning a child assigns to his collective relationships. We need not feel threatened by the beauty he finds in others, past or present. His finding beauty in those veins enriches him. If we truly believe he is a part of us, then we know that his enrichment enriches us. His intimacy with people and culture not *of* us and ours is in fact a central ingredient in his intimacy *with* us and ours.

The idea that we may compensate for original family is a myth we wrap around our minds to comfort us from the reality that there is no compensation. That hole left by the original cannot be filled except by the original. Even then, time moves the grains of sand too fast and far for there ever to be a complete filling of the hole. We need not go on trying to fill holes to which we do not belong. Our place is to fill the broader holes of love and compassion, of understanding and validation that this world burnishes into a gaping abyss.

The child is not conflicted about original family. We are. The child then becomes conflicted about our conflict. His natural drive is to suck from his original roots. It is our conflict, and his protectiveness toward our conflict, that prevents him from accessing his roots. Love is not to be parceled out so that a child must deduct love from one family in order to increase love for another family. This is what our conflict speaks to the child. This is a mad interpretation of life that we offer him as dessert to the main course of our fears. He is perfectly capable of integrating love for each aspect of his whole into his heart if we would only stop forcing fractions into his mind. This is what makes our child welfare unnatural.

We fill our children with guilt and shame over their unavoidable yearnings for original family and heritage. In the new families we make, we sign pacts of silence and disavowing pertaining to original family. In doing so we have constructed additions to the home where no one is allowed to venture. Those additions are always drafty and a cold wind blows into the part of the home we occupy. Our children sleep in these drafts, they awaken to these drafts, they come home from hurtful days at school only to be chilled again by these drafts. How are they to find warmth in such a home?

The natural world does not seek to destroy roots or chop up children's hearts into parts for a possession-puzzle. Children die sure as butterflies from the closing fist of their landing place. Love does not close down upon beauty, it opens up to it. It does not seek to cut beauty off from its first roots; it nourishes those roots so that the flower may bloom endlessly. Love is wonderfully selfish in the way that it feeds beauty. What starves beauty is not love. We have to stop killing our child's roots with our conflict. Let us turn the extermination toward our own killing pulse.

Children often need protection from unhealthy aspects of their original family. This in no way needs to conflict with us helping them to develop a positive sense of their roots. When we kill off a child's connection with these roots we are killing off her connection to self.

We can create a positive image of an original parent even if that parent has caused harm. This is an opportunity to help the child learn about the complexity of being human. She needs to know that no one is a one-dimensional cartoon character. We all have flaws and weaknesses. This insight is a basis for her to avoid developing a prejudiced mind and heart. Even if a hurtful monster dwells in her original parents, she need not grow up believing she is the offspring of monsters.

We can instill in her a positive sense about her broader family even if members of her family are living shameful lives. There is no reason why we cannot conceive along with her that her ancestors were beautiful people. Why steal from her the idea that she comes from beauty? If we are so loathing and scornful of everything she comes from perhaps we should not be the ones to have her in our life. Our hatred and animosity toward her roots will reach her. Those energies cannot be hidden. She will feel this and suffer. Her attachment to us will be corroded. Her esteem damaged. She will endlessly question whether or not she belongs with us. If we have these feelings, we have work to do.

Why not create, with her, positive, realistic stories about the community from which she comes? Surely there is abundant beauty in every community. If we personally struggle with this, it may be a sign of how deeply prejudice has seeped into us. There is no child of whom we can rightly say: *There is nothing good about what she comes from. To protect her we must erase her family, community, and heritage from her mind and heart.* No such child exists:

Many of us believe deep inside
that when we acquire a child
the child is our possession

even in birth a child is not our possession
she is not ours in ownership
she is with us
she is for us
she is not us

nor a slave
she is not owned
she has a throne
built ages before she
pierced this world
so long before she came to us
and even if she came through us
her task is not to do us
be us
cower to us
but see through us
to her purpose all a blush

we have made a carnival
out of a most natural thing
disruption is inherent in life

no family is an exception
children drift and falter
adults gravitate
meet the child at compassion's alter
together they kneel in surrender
to life's perfect chaos

palms forming forever-flowers
make promises to one another
involving faint steps toward each other
and toward the commandment
Thou Shalt Not Smother This Divine Soul
in the clammy air of their fear expelled

no
our child welfare is not natural
legal bindings hold no weight
where children seek the truth
within their fate
and too the apex of their belonging

embrace is not a legal song
it is a dream that comes at night
taking young beside a pond
where turtles stack themselves
on one another so that each may taste
the glow of sun

and quiet ducks of emerald crown
arch their graceful necks to clean their down

and parades of ripples stride the water
and leaf beds billow each time a lover
in wind touches down

this dream every sprout spends childhood
walking through is a dream of honesty
of nakedness of beautiful things
finding each other and not lying
not crushing not controlling not defining
not deceiving not avoiding not denying

each earthquake is the aftershock
of every child crying
each sunrise is the pouring
of a billion buttercup bouquets
sweetened by a child unyoked
and flying

that gentle breeze?
nature sighing
relieved that we let go
let her go
a feather free
becoming.

CULTURAL NEGOTIATION

A family is a symphony. Each member must play her instrument at an optimal level for a virtuoso performance. This requires reciprocity. The culture of a family who embraces a dislocated child is preexisting. The child's culture is less developed, stable, and secure. It requires more validation. Who is being asked to make what accommodations? Parents need also to admit their own need for validation. Change creates insecurity in all ages.

Any group is an ongoing negotiation of cultural essence. Our families and communities are such bodies. The selling of commodities is a part of this negotiation. Some groups do their bartering silently, others boisterously and with clamor. However the manner, we best negotiate collective group values by honoring and validating personal values. This is not to be avoided without conflict. Treading over personal values on the way to setting group values can produce dire consequences in a young heart that has been denied. Not only have we denied her, we have insulted her own way of being.

When we embrace each other in our lives, this should be a mutual embrace. It costs us nothing to nurture each other's personal culture. As we look into the lives of the happiest people, we see they are the ones who receive the most daily internal massages. We have the power to become our loved ones' favorite masseuses.

We should understand that our relationship with a child is a two-way street. Mutual change is required or pathology will be at hand. We can be patient with a child's adjustment, can't we? How long did it take us to adjust to our marriage? To our new job or community? Even 18-year-olds can take a couple of years to adjust to college. Imagine what a young child goes through being embraced into our new family or community *campus*.

Her transition into our life involves a broader web. The world we bring her into is not bounded by a physical home. Extended family and the community are meaningful cultural elements into which she is also transitioning. If we are wise, we will be considerate and perceptive of the broader cultural immersion she is going through, no matter her background. We will create beautiful music and we will do so together.

SEGREGATED HOMES AND LIVES

Does the evidence of a child's heritage and culture that decorates her bedroom end at her bedroom door? Is the rest of your home vacant of this evidence? If so, you have a segregated home on your hands. The message to her is glaring: *We love you and honor who you are, but only so far as your bedroom. The rest of this house, the main part of who we are does not receive you, has not integrated you, is no reflection of you.* Every day she walks through this domain she is blistered with rejection by this obvious absence.

The same discordant note is struck when the cultural flavor of her social life finds no kindred spirit in your social life. Now you have built a segregated life. You and your family are a ground into which she wishes to put her roots. But first she must find evidence that her roots are welcome. She is looking for certain familiar artifacts but the ground is barren. Segregated homes, lives, and classrooms are not decent invitations to become one—family, friendship, community. They are instead a false embrace. She has made the effort to incorporate who we are into her way of being. Where is our response? Reciprocity is a necessary seed for bonding and trust.

DIVERSITY

Diversity is a word we greatly misuse. This has caused many people to take a dismissive, smug attitude. Diversity has nothing to do with numbers and quotas. It has everything to do with the nature of relationship between objects, toward greater productivity and health.

All we need to do is pay attention to life itself to see that diversity is a fundamental law of nature. Financiers diversify; teams diversify; educators diversify; farmers diversify; investors diversify; life diversifies. All these elements benefit greatly from true diversity. Such infusion creates balance and optimizes flow. Why would our objective with children not be to diversify their identities into wholeness? Why would we not diversify the growth stimulants to which we expose them? Why would we not diversify our own social circle that our children have no choice but to swim in?

Diversity is the nature of life. It is not charity we do for certain groups. It is the act of becoming greater, divorcing singularity and impotence, increasing our fertility along any dimension. Participating in the undeniable diverse nature of life is a choice we make for our own sake, not as a favor to others. We need to spend real time thinking about this, and change our mental associations with the concept. Our youth rely upon our re-education.

This social world is our drinking water. Do we pollute our water with prejudice and cloistering or do we purify it with flow? Sitting water grows rancid. Nature tells us this. Our social world is also our air. Do we close ourselves and suffocate or open ourselves and breathe? We must ask what crops have we planted in this child. A child is a treasure of land. What we plant, water, feed, nourish, give sunlight becomes our harvest. We do reap what we sow.

And as our harvest emerges, do we let parts of its essence rot from neglect, or do we bring its wholeness to our table? Our children are screaming in code to have their completeness be let completely inside.

A family can contain seven people of seven distinct ethnicities and still be extremely lacking in diversity. Again, diversity is not a function of quantities. It is the active honoring of culture through healthy, reciprocal relationships. Diversity when honored and active creates family flexibility, resilience, and resourcefulness.

As part of an honoring habit we identify collective and personal strengths and challenges. We learn to talk about roles in a complementary way. Traditions and rituals solidify these honorable habits in our daily life. Families who resist the often challenging task of learning to honor their latent diversity are simply making a plea to us: *Show us the rewards for honoring diversity.* We do not have far to look. The trophy cabinet is stocked.

If we are truly devoted to providing a child an infusion of cultural variety into our homogenous home or community, we will act. We can always encourage diverse relationships, in his life and ours. If we are brave and recognize our interdependency, other possibilities open up to us. We may honestly consider moving from our homogenous community into one that better reflects his nature or heritage.

Why are so many of us prepared to have our child suffer severe cultural isolation but so completely afraid of tasting a degree of that ourselves? If the idea is so frightening to us, this should be a doorway for considering how difficult it is for him. He is young and supposedly more vulnerable than we are. Can our compassion motivate us to creatively achieve diversity? If so, we are well on our way. Creativity is an abundant and potent stream in each of us. With the will, we can find a way.

If we do not choose to move to another community, we can travel at every feasible opportunity. We can go to the world if the world is not able to penetrate our insulated environment. We can have him visit with relatives, friends, and mentors in other, more diverse communities. We can role model relationship-building for him by stretching ourselves to meet new people in varied situations. None of us is completely restricted in the ways we can open up his and our life to the beautiful infusion of variety. We require only a reason.

The groups we seek out for him to join do not always have to be thematically tied to his separation experience. Groups in general can be good for his growth and for the distinctive aspects of his identity. If we diversify the activities in which he is involved, the branches of his wholeness are tended to. He fills out.

If children come from a heritage that is barely represented in their current environment, feelings of isolation are almost inevitable. Cultural isolation stifles their story and song. Perhaps the few available adults of their heritage have social roles defined as menial or lesser by the immediate mainstream culture. This can send a dehumanizing message to our youth.

A common example is when the only people in youths' lives of their same heritage are janitors, secretaries, maids, maintenance workers, gardeners, etc. These are roles that do not receive the respect they deserve. When we allow such people to remain in the background and periphery, silent and uninvited to the main flow, we injure children who identify themselves as being somehow a part of these undervalued human beings.

We need to humanize these good people with whom our youth share a distinctive heritage. Why aren't more of these workers invited to share their life stories in our children's classes at school? Often they work at those same schools and still we allow them to remain neglected shadows, invisible servants. We can assert our desire to have their work, lives, and beauty celebrated in the presence of our children. This is called being invested in the ones we care about. This is how we wrap our young in social safety blankets.

HOW A CHILD DEFINES *SAFETY*

Reflect on a relationship in your life in which you have felt safe to be yourself, share yourself, and receive and give love. What qualities did that relationship possess? Your list of traits is a nice blueprint for what you can build in your relationship with an uprooted child; and what you can help the child build in the relationships of his life.

Now reflect on a relationship in your life in which you have felt unsafe to be yourself, share yourself, and receive and give love. What exactly caused you to feel this way? It is very likely that the same components ail this child. This is a simple way to increase our understanding of youth safety: by reflecting on our own relationships.

Safe spaces for a child are those that contain the same elements as reflection ponds: stillness, clarity, honesty, compassion, understanding, patience, consistency. In safe spaces a child knows she can live her truth and not be slapped for it—literally or otherwise. She knows she does not have to imitate other's beauty—she can cast out her own. In her safe spaces she can relax and let all of the world pour into her. This is her whole self, her big self flowing into her. A safe space is not defined by what we adults assume should leave her feeling safe. A safe space is defined by her *feeling* safe. No higher qualification exists.

An overwhelming majority of uprooted children come from loving homes. Some have been treated horrifically, but even many of those were loved. Surely there is a payoff when we find children a more stable environment. But if that new environment contains its own form of abuse, neglect, denial—however subtle—now we have exposed children to a succession of wounds.

This cascade of continual injury to their dignity and worth is a slippery surface to walk. Each wound may be more severe than the previous, simply due to the exponential nature of woundedness. Wounds do not add on to one another. They multiply in collective impact.

So many children would die if they could only have a moment of feeling safe in the world. So many children do die, feeling that is their only way to feel safe in the world. Who has led them to this precipice?

TURTLES ON THE BEACH

When baby sea turtles break forth from their egg shells in their dune nests on the beach, their defining task is to make it safely to the water. At this point, there are no grown turtles to protect them. Along their trek to safety are many dangers. Some are predictable, others cruel in their randomness. The physical distance from birth to safety might seem fairly short to our eyes. To the baby turtle the distance does not end. As with children, peril lengthens the turtles' perception of safety's nearness.

Some of the baby turtles become flipped over on their backsides and bake in the uncaring sun. Others are eaten by predators. Driftwood blocks their route. Like the baby turtles, the path our children perceive between their unsafe reality and someplace secure is winding and treacherous. The path is a funhouse hallway. With every step forward it seems to our young that the endpoint moves farther back, away from them, taunting their efforts. Our self-focused attitudes and counterproductive habits become the sun scalding our young on their way to the water. The ones who become flipped over on their backs, the ones who have faltered, burn the worst. Where is the shade they need? How can we provide it? Life's circumstance becomes their driftwood. Can we drag those barriers off the beach? If not, we have to help our young climb over. Our prejudice becomes their predator. If we wish to rid their path of deadly stalkers we may need to go on a hunting trip within our own hearts and minds. Turtle-child eaters love to prowl in those internal woods.

Those of us who fervently believe we have no prejudice regarding our children are so often the ones who do the most harm. Our blind spots batter youth. They have no recourse. When you take your grievances to a king who believes he does no wrong, your case is likely to go unheard. Worse, you may end up in the dungeon.

Children of certain descent represent the groups toward which their society has historically held the greatest degree of animosity, hostility, and dehumanizing values. Their sense of safety in life is likely to derive largely from their sense that their family values their historically scorned heritage. They need to know their family feels good about their heritage, and is devoted to understanding their heritage. Ultimately, their feelings of safety depend on knowing that the people closest to them are faithfully willing to protect and stand up for the integrity of their heritage, their essence, their story.

All uprooted children share this need to have their distinction embraced. For many of these children, the concept of safety at home extends in important ways beyond mainstream concepts of shelter, sustenance, guidance, and love. These children need to know that their internal dismay has a place to forever rest its weariness.

His heart journal:

I exist
behind the blinding mist
your prejudice
casts upon my bliss
look deeper and discover
I exist.

CREATING SAFE SPACES

Safe spaces are composed of mutual sharing and mutual seeing. Each person is devoted to honoring the other, confident that the infusion will be returned reciprocally. Mutuality becomes a tradition, a reflexive way of interacting that fosters intimacy and bonding.

These spaces involve compassionate listening. This is listening without judgment, without interruption. Compassion has a special way of seeing things. The listener is fully present and open, receiving everything being shared. The mind is not split, with half of it listening and the other half drifting, defending, or preparing a response. Children can feel us truly listening, absorbing. Compassionate listening motivates further sharing. It feels good to be received.

Youth labeled as non-communicative will spill their treasure to someone who makes them feel that the content of their offering is deeply desired. It is not enough for us to want children to talk. We must want to receive what their talking produces. Compassionate listening has clear goals: validating and affirming what lies in the speaker's heart. Compassionate listening does not criticize, even as it offers helpful feedback and alternative ways of seeing. This kind of listening is not primarily concerned with the self. It is confident that by caring for the speaker its own needs will be addressed in return.

Safe spaces contain loving speech. This is not syrupy language. It is genuine warmth and nurturance. It soothes and massages the beauty within a listening child, even as it corrects or guides her. Loving speech is received as a gentle if firm breeze, not as a sledgehammer. Children look forward to listening to loving speech. They tune out harsh, demeaning speech the moment it leaves the lips.

Within child-safe spaces adults are honest in their assessment of their fears, biases, and prejudices. They acknowledge these barriers to youth. Adults become storytellers, explaining to children how they acquired these thoughts and feelings. Trust builds in the youth— they at least know they are dealing with someone honest and genuine. They do not have to wonder whether or not they are being deceived.

Inside safe spaces we adults freely ask our youth to help us understand. We say to them: *Teach me.* And we mean it. The statement is a prompt for a child to express herself. It gives her the floor and lets her know we will not jump all over what she says. We are humble students. This empowers her, gives her a sense of control. She is not used to feeling in control around adults, many of whom condescend to her. This is feeling good. She wants more. She looks forward to meeting us and sharing in the safe space we have created together.

Her heart journal: *I am a pebble bouncing between boulders who believe they are stroking me with feathers. Their touch feels like stone.*

LOSS AND ABANDONMENT

There is a primacy to healing. Separated youth have inherently experienced some kind of loss and abandonment. We are often motivated to minimize this loss. A child's lasting pain discomforts us. We want him to heal and become normal now that he is out of his past circumstance and with us. We want this badly for him. Truthfully, the longer he shows signs of woundedness the more it drains us. Our heart is invested in being patient and supportive, but eventually we expect to return to normalcy together.

What we may not realize is that our relationship may hinge on the way in which we allow his healing. The magnitude of his pain is real and valid. He has been impacted in a way that cares nothing for our timetable. If we underestimate the impact of his loss we are likely to misidentify the meaning of his behavior.

Loss is relative. There is a significant difference between being willfully abandoned and being deprived of family by an uncontrollable fate. A child's mind has a way of making sense of trauma such that these two means of separation begin to look alike, begin to live alike in his mind. Guilt mushrooms in his tear-moistened heart. He blames himself for what went wrong. He labels himself as worthless and ugly. He hangs the banner of shame on his face and posture. What actually happened becomes clouded in his reconstruction of reality. That truth may take many years for him to retrieve.

Some separation is slow, chronic. Other loss is sudden, acute. Both can lead to trauma. Both are capable of carving deep canyons in the heart. To a child, separation from people we have labeled as *good* is no more inherently hurtful than separation from those we would label *bad*. Losing family to a tragic accident is not necessarily more hurtful than loss caused by the failings of loved ones. Losing family by death is not always a more pronounced loss than losing family by dislocation or dishonor.

We project our personal values onto a child's loss and presume what his loss should mean to him. We categorize the nature of his loss and use those categories to build our expectations of his response to the loss. Entire schemas and maps for his healing journey play out in our minds. This dictates our patience, frustration, and subtle interplay with his healing persona.

All of this projection and presumption comes from a compassionate heart. But it is dealt from our often illusory mental deck. How he experiences his loss is a phenomenon dictated by his uniqueness. We may have previews from the world around us. But the main feature that is his healing remains mysterious even as it unfolds.

One of the greatest medicines we can offer him is the work we do to resist building our temples of expectation. We can be guaranteed that he will not feel safe going to those temples to nurture his transformation. One day, though, he will come running to the free space of our non-dictation. A heart that needs to breathe will go where it is allowed to take a breath.

Healing from loss must occur as part of a child's attachment processes. We should not expect healing from loss to be complete before attachment begins. The two streams are interdependent functions of one another.

He needs for us to not relate to him as a broken vessel. Not everything he struggles with is due to his loss. A key is to strike a balance between his loss experience and his present and future reality. Our symphony together is built upon such keys of balance and moderation.

He is the authority of his loss. He is the author of his experience. He should be the one to dictate the storytelling that is done relative to his loss. This depends on the presence of a safe *space* and permission (his and ours) for grieving. His loss should not be muted from family life and culture but woven into the quilt of normalcy. In every one of his relationships loss has been experienced by each person. How the respective stories are told, received, and honored, shapes his healing and ours.

In our eagerness to create normal lives for separated children, we sometimes do not allow them the space to lick their wounds. In nature, an animal licking its wounds is not as trivial as it may seem to us. The licking applies saliva to the wound, dousing it in sanitizing bacteria that prevents infection. This is the act of direct healing. The context is that the animal requires solitude, a safe space to let down its guard and focus on its healing. Most of all, it seeks consideration from its family and community that it is wounded and requires this special time.

As humans we also require certain things for our self-healing: solitude, social support, privacy, the voicing of our story, reflection, affirmation, validation, stillness, safety, security, and the will to heal.

How many times has a child tried to express something to us—her story? How many times has our reaction had the effect of saying to her: *Go rewrite the script?* What she has to express can have no editors, only listeners and interpreters. If we continue to reject what she has to tell us, she may stop coming to us to tell it. Worse, she may cease trying to write her script. Now she is the songbird who lets the melody die inside.

When children tell their stories, however lovingly, but with a necessary honesty, so often we reply with bitterness, anger, resentment. Our own fester rises as a geyser to drown out and invalidate their voice. All because we cannot stand to have them point out our own failings:

our lack of perfection in vanquishing their pain. We lash out at children who are simply trying utterly to express how life and we have affected them.

The root of our lashing out is that the very notion of our imperfection threatens our sense that we are good. Our goodness is the buoy we cling to desperately in the sea of life. It is the one concept we cannot surrender without dying a certain death. This lashing out at children whose pain points the way to our own imperfection is an irony of self-defeatism. Acknowledging our imperfection increases our goodness. There is no threat to our goodness in what children share.

SURVIVOR'S GUILT

Children can experience a pervasive guilt when their lives improve away from original family, regardless of how the family they left behind fares. Children's natural tendency is to blame themselves for being separated. They may feel they abandoned their family, in spite of the actual facts. They are burdened with an acute awareness that their leaving caused pain in loved ones, friends, and peers.

The sense of survivor's guilt sharpens when family and friends left behind continue to suffer from addiction, war, poverty, famine, and the like. As we expect children newly in our midst to exhale great gusts of relief and gratitude for their recent blessings, they contend with the separation that led them to those blessings.

If we slay a thousand souls on the way to finding drinking water in the desert, the cool, fresh water barely registers in our mouths. We are consumed instead with mourning the pain we believe we have caused others, the suffering we have left behind. This is our children. We throw them a party; expect them to celebrate their good fortune. They dig deep to smile hard, to please us. They are happy for their fortune. But their heart still mourns.

In our house, in our arms, in our society of human kind, do we force them to retreat to the closet in the middle of the party so they can cry their tears? What space do we give them for their mourning? When do we allow them to not be happy? When do they get to feel and see us being content with the unglamorous blessing that they are still making an effort to join us in our world?

MOVING THROUGH TRAUMA

The landscape a child navigates in moving through her trauma toward wholeness and health can be imagined as a mountainous jungle choking-thick with trees. As she struggles to cut through the denseness, she has a couple of natural elements to orient her in the right direction: sunlight and water. The nature of this jungle is that it contains streams that eventually become rivers. Those rivers all flow toward the sea. The sea is her destination. It is the water of her healing and fulfillment. If she can find and follow a stream it will one day lead her to a river. She can navigate that river until it joins with the sea.

The closer she gets to the sea, the more the landscape will change. The denseness will retreat. The trees will open up farther and farther, allowing her more space and granting her less resistance. The precariously steep slope will flatten out, giving her firmer footing for her journey. She will begin to smell the scent of the sea, the scent of well-being. The closer she is to health, the more she recognizes the signs of being healthy.

Sunlight allows her to see through the dark, shadowed stretches beneath the jungle's canopy. The more light she is afforded the better her sense of judgment. She can discern shapes and forms with greater accuracy. As long as she has light she has a chance. We provide her a measure of light through our nurturing, compassionate relationship with her. We light her path when we truly listen to her. She is showered in light when her true beauty is noticed, celebrated, and made use of by others. Friendship, stability, honesty—all these elements are forms of light to help her see through the darkness.

For some children, smiling betrays the pseudo-stability of clinging to pain. To smile sends warm tendrils of possibility through the cold exterior of a calloused heart. This is threatening. Possibility is a fragile thing. Under a morose mental shade, a child who extends herself toward possibility risks being crushed yet again. We may love to see a smiling child. It soothes us. She may be haunted by the fright of smiling. Sometimes, maybe for a certain season, she needs us to let her frown.

Sometimes the pain becomes too much. The sympathetic mind wraps the heart in a blanket of numbness so that it will not have to feel. This is how many youth survive their horrors. They become zombies and ghosts. They are not fully present any longer in this world where pain can reach them. Going through the motions, they make it through. It is all they can do. Numbness is a survival reflex. It gets them through the painful moments.

Like us, they believe that they can get away with burying their emotions and memories. Over time they realize that buried pain is a rat fanatically clawing at the box they have buried it in. A creature with sharp claws has been tearing at them for years. At some point they realize the only way to be free of this suffering is to set the clawing pain free.

They begin to gingerly let the emotions and memories, their story, squeeze out through their heart and mind barriers. If they are fortunate, they have someone skilled at this as midwife to the birth. If they are fortunate again, the thin ribbon of flow they allow opens into a river and deep healing occurs. This can be a messy birth but it is the death of suffering. This unburying is a long chore over many seasons for our children. Can we find the proper means to coax out their buried story?

DIRTY WATER

When we turn off the water pipes to do plumbing work we have an understanding. After some time has passed we turn the pipes back on again. When we then turn on the faucet in the sink and the water runs out it is often brown, muddy, dirty. We are not alarmed. We understand that the water is discolored because of the work that we have done on the plumbing system. The discoloring tells us that repairs have occurred. Our understanding lets us know that eventually the rustiness will wash out of the pipes and the water will run clean again.

When a boy begins to express himself creatively, in writing, drawing, or some other manner, dirty water may run out from his heart. Anger, gloom, and despair can spew out in such a strong, dark stream. This disturbs and worries us. Sometimes our concern is valid and necessary. We should remember, though, our faucet after the plumbing work. What comes out of the young man now may be evidence that a blockage has been loosened or dissolved. This may be a sign that work has been done. He is flowing again. As he continues to express himself and liberate his feelings, his water may eventually turn clear.

Our understanding of this process is what will prompt us to allow him to continue pouring out dirty water for a while. Without this understanding our fear and concern may lead us to pounce on his creative expression and criticize what he has done. In doing so, we stop the very stream that was beginning to cleanse him. Sometimes dirty water is a good sign that something pure and clean is on the way.

CANARIES IN THE COAL MINE

We can learn much from nature and each of its creatures. The relationship between humans and canaries may seem peculiar and distant but in the context of coal mines the intimacy between the two comes shining forth. In the old days coal miners would take canaries in cages with them down into the dark mines far beneath the Earth. That far down, toxic fumes can easily accumulate in the closed spaces of the mines. Our human senses are not equipped to detect these deadly gases. When they build up, miners can be quickly overcome. Thousands of deaths and near deaths have occurred because of this.

Here is where the role of the canaries becomes clear. Out in the world we appear to have little need for something as small as a canary. But in the coal mine they become invaluable to the miner. Everything is priceless in the right context. Canaries are much more sensitive than we are to the kinds of deadly gases that can build up deep in the Earth's belly. Knowing this, the miners would keep the canaries close by in their cages.

When the canaries stopped singing, this was an alarm to the miners of a possible emergency with the gases. When the canaries began to sway, then fall over and die, this was a certain sign to the miners that they had better get out of the mine as soon as possible. For although the gases had not yet built up to a level concentrated enough to begin making the miners sick, they knew eventually they too could be overtaken and killed.

This simple understanding the miners had for the nature of canaries allowed them to prevent some illness and death among the workers. Unfortunately, they sacrificed many canaries along the way. This relationship provides us a very obvious allegory through which to view our way of relating to children.

We have an opportunity to view separated children as canaries who have been made more sensitive or allergic to certain life elements that are unhealthy to all of us. We often view these children as tainted and their behavior and attitudes as entirely negative. We interpret their distinctiveness from other children as evidence that they are dysfunctional. What if we viewed their lack of song, their acting out, their struggle, as their canary-warning to us that unhealthy elements exist in their lives and ours?

The question is whether or not we view their behavior and attitudes as dysfunction or allergy. While certainly much of what they express can be counterproductive, this does not mean that they alone possess the dysfunction in question. They might just be the loudest at protesting a dysfunction that is epidemic in their social circle.

Holistic approaches tell us that when seeking to cure what ails a child, we should seek first to recognize what ails the water from which the child drinks, the food the child eats, the air the child breathes, the relationships in which the child is encumbered. Too often we become fixated on a child as the source and location of the problem. The locale of the dysfunction more often lies within a child's collective life space. To treat the child we must treat the collective.

Rather than pathologizing our children, developing a habit of seeing them as perpetually flawed, we have an alternative. It may be much more productive to think of a child as a *vessel* vulnerable to what flows *through* her. We—the child's family, friends, teachers, therapists, community—are also vessels, with our own rivers running through us. Perhaps a traumatized child is like the child who has developed an allergy and is now more sensitive to the allergens that exist, not within her but around her. Perhaps we are vessels who unwittingly deliver certain allergens to the child. The potential culprits are numerous:

◊ Forced change
◊ Destructive authority
◊ Power abuse
◊ Condescension
◊ Sympathy
◊ Low expectations
◊ Lack of empathy
◊ Harmful expectations
◊ Impatience
◊ Smothering control
◊ Anger

◊ Anxiety
◊ Rigid interaction
◊ Blocked communication
◊ Prejudice
◊ Judgmental attitudes
◊ Dishonesty
◊ Fear
◊ Avoidance
◊ Denial
◊ Our own pain
◊ Our own dysfunction

None of these dysfunctions is healthy to us. But as adults many of us have developed a greater capacity to tolerate them. This does not mean we are not becoming sickened by these pollutants just as our children are. They, vulnerable canaries that they are, might just stop chirping (thriving) before we do. Can we imagine our own lives as being lived in the precarious space that is a coal mine? All these noxious elements of society are silently, invisibly accumulating in our midst. The buildup is causing us anxiety, disease, anger, detachment. Does this sound familiar? Does this realization of our personal coal mine cause us to look upon children in a brighter light?

Maybe, when we vessels, carrying all these allergens, attempt to place our arms around a traumatized child, her sensitized system is alarmed and overwhelmed by the allergen stowaways in our embrace. Maybe her troubling behavior and attitudes are her allergic inflammation. We must stop assuming stigmatized children are the locus (location) or source of the problem.

Yes, children carry traumas within them from their past. But even in their present lives with us we are introducing them to new traumas. Maybe they are less obvious traumas but traumas just the same. We should view trauma as a *shared wound* within a child's life web, an aggregation of insults to the child.

Trauma creates attachment wounds (wounds leading to detachment). But what lies at the crux of helping a child is not the acuteness of a particular attachment wound. Rather it is the sum or aggregate of attachment wounds that exist in the holistic life arena of the child. Those collective wounds are both our treatment target and our treatment avenue.

Perhaps we should initiate our preventions and interventions by first reconceptualizing trauma. We can view trauma as a shared wound, manifesting as a system of vessels, whose locations we may find scattered like a quilt throughout a child's social circle. This might position us onto an entirely new creative track in embracing children. Our creativity would open up like a geyser if we imagined children and their wounds as a function of our life together and the wounds we bring into their orbit.

Children can experience therapeutic attention as highlighting *what's wrong with me*, rather than *what's wrong in my life*. This can rupture esteem, create stigma, invade privacy, and aggravate a child's defensive impulse for self-protection. We can avoid this by focusing on the holistic situation involved, rather than the child as the source of flaw, problem, or trouble.

At the same time, we highlight how the child strengthens her family, her social circle, her school. As a team, we address with her ways *to improve upon a challenge area*, rather than *to cure a problem* within her. If our habit is to take the onus off her tendency to criticize herself and place it on her social circle, we disperse pressure. We lighten the weight she carries.

Separated children are truly canaries in the coal mine. Because of their life experiences, they have become more allergic, more sensitive to the harmful social energies and attitudes that sicken us all. Beauty and worth can be drawn from children's sensitivities. We should listen when these canaries sing!

Her heart journal: *People want to solve my problems. People are my problems. They need to solve themselves.*

INSTINCT AND IMPULSE

In the open desert there is no shade. The punishing heat creates mirages of the mind and vision. The things we are dying for magically appear. We so dearly desire water and there it is, in that lagoon that has just blossomed so incredibly before us. Uprooted children walk their own punishing desert. What they are desperate for has a way of appearing before them as illusion. Their hearts and spirits want certain things so badly that their minds acquiesce.

A girl who offers or exposes herself sexually in harmful ways is walking her own private desert, seeking the waters of affection, love, validation. We must give her real water, not these mirages. Her real water comes in the form of healthy relationships that honor her true beauty.

The boy who is enticed by street gangs is thirsty for something: Belonging. Identity. Protection. Status. He is delirious in his state of aloneness. A street gang appears before him as an attractive, welcoming family. His eyes dazzled wide, his awareness sleeping, he walks through the door that he believes will bring him home.

We must fill his life with the substance of his true thirst. When he drinks from watering holes that do not actually exist, his thirst is unabated. He continues gravitating toward other harmful mirages. Once he drinks from the substance of things that quench his true thirst, he becomes satiated. In this state, he no longer needs to harm himself wandering. His desert becomes rich with shade trees, places to rest.

A nexus or link exists between *instinct* (healthy and of the spirit) and *impulse* (often unhealthy and born of pain, fear, anxiety, insecurity, and unmet need). When a young girl feels the need to be loved and reacts by expressing herself sexually, her need to be loved is her instinct, and it is healthy. Seeking to fill this need sexually is an impulse, and in this case, very unhealthy. Within this space of translation from instinct to impulse we may offer helpful guidance to our children and youth. We can teach them how to recognize their healthy instincts, their unhealthy impulses, and how to distinguish between them.

Receptor cells in our bodies allow one molecule to bond with another. Children have receptor cells of their own: instinct. Instinct when operating properly allows children to receive and manifest such dynamic molecules as trust, faith, security, personal esteem, group esteem, self-concept, self-worth, continuity of relationships, self-forgiveness, forgiveness, contradictions within love, compassion, empathy, respect, honor, the imperfections of learning, and imperfections in general. In sum, healthy instinct allows children to receive and manifest health itself—a circular and self-perpetuating chain.

When damaged or blocked, children's receptor cells of instinct become like the clogged fuel injectors of a vehicle. The vital and healthy molecules of being a social human become trapped within youthful vessels. A backup develops. The vital material is blocked from flowing into children and out from children into others. When any healthy material is released from youth it has become so pressurized that it often releases in explosive outbursts of energy, emotion, and thoughts. In fact, it has now become so distorted by pressure that it can also be released in ways that are obsessive, compulsive, exaggerated, repetitive, angry, and/or desperate. This is how even essentially healthy feelings and thoughts can become transformed into dysfunction as they are expressed.

Youth often follow their healthy instinct for acceptance in a social group but stumble impulsively into criminal behavior. Instinct is the voice of true culture. Impulse can be the voice of superficial culture. Young people frequently exaggerate the signs and symbols of their group affiliations through clothing, hairstyles, music, and behavior. This is because impulses by nature involve exaggerated or magnified bursts of representing the self. We should understand that our young are seeking their true culture and the paths available are largely decorated with superficial culture.

We have a role to play here. We can guide them toward the true culture they seek by helping them open up their blocked instinct channels. This requires the healing of their instinct-receptor cells. Self-awareness beckons.

THE SELF-HEALING CHILD

A child without a clear, accurate identity or recognition of her place in the web of life cannot direct herself, cannot heal herself, cannot nurture herself. To expect that our institutions can ultimately heal a child is a great deception.

Only the child can heal herself. At most we become facilitators of her healing; we help to provide setting, nourishment, a road map, support, and encouragement. She must take the actual steps along her path. This means that in order to shepherd her we must know something of her nature and of her path. We have no choice but to go on a journey of discovering her many textures.

How else do we as institutions help create self-healing, self-direction, and self-nurturance? We adults who are the embodiment of our institutions do so by acquiring those capacities ourselves. Then we teach those skills and mentalities to children through modeling, storytelling, and practice. By being a reflection of what a whole person looks like we activate children's wholeness.

Children desperately need an inner life. We all do. Our children live in a world that buzzes and blurs with stress and stimulus. They are raced from one responsibility to the next from waking till bedtime. Even in their sleep they anxiously work through the burdens on their chest. If they have no time to be alone within themselves, that undone inner work will leave them failing at the great life assignment called peace.

Rarely being alone, they will develop a discomfort at being alone. Scarcely ever taking internal inventory, their spirits become cluttered, blocked, and stifled. We can tell when our homes need spring cleaning. Can we also notice that our children need regular cleansing? They cannot get away with living an entirely external life. Their sacred self needs maintenance and polishing. We can teach them these habits by blessing ourselves with the same.

Children are vulnerable to a piercing helplessness. In this space they feel as though they have been hollowed out, emptied of any meaningful abilities or worth. The more they view themselves as broken, at risk, and impoverished, the greater their dependency. Chief Crow spoke these words: *In you are natural powers. You already possess everything you need to be great.*

These words are a drumbeat we should sing children to sleep with each night. Hearing this proclamation throughout their early seasons, something is bound to seep through the rock surface of their poor esteem and reach their softness: *In me are natural powers. In me are natural powers. I was born great.* These ideas produce hope and confidence. They are seed for many proud becomings.

RESILIENCE

Resilience is not the capacity to survive. It is the capacity to thrive. Many souls walk the Earth alive without truly living. They are vacant, running on the fumes of instinct, barely going through the motions. Our expectation must be that youth thrive, that their spirits be active, their creativity surging, their lust for living ripe on the vine. Nothing short of this will make our generations fertile.

A child's spirit is by nature a force of freedom. In its healthy state it never stops yearning to reach its peak blossom and astound the world with its glory.

A child's inherent strength of being, her natural capacity to endure and cope, is not the sole determinant of whether or not she will survive, much less heal and thrive. Even the strongest child will drown in the ocean of life if the undertow is powerful enough and if she does not have something to hold on to so she can resist the current.

The most resilient child is not the most intelligent, attractive, positive, or likable. She is not the most successful in school or even the most loved. The most resilient child is the one who has the most reason to live. Reason and purpose create the desire to live. When her blood is filled with the corpuscles of desire and will, she is capable of thriving even through the greatest horror. She lives not only for herself but to fulfill the clarion call of something outside of herself. Her life has meaning. There is a point to her struggle.

We model purpose for her by living purposeful lives. It is not enough that we act out the script. We need to narrate for her the point of our actions and decisions. We need to tell the story of how we are responding to purpose.

Our fingers should point out life's play. A natural recipe for resilience unfolds all around her. The resilient trees are those with the strongest intact roots that extend deep or wide; roots that are open vessels to extract nutrition from the wholeness that is Earth. Resilient buildings have the sturdiest foundations. Resilient relationships have open, flowing communication. Resilient livestock and crops contain genetic diversity. The recipe is not a mystery. Life is showing us in every moment how to make this meal.

Don't put all your eggs in one basket. This is a well known saying that speaks to resilience. It is likely the saying emerged because one day someone tripped and broke all the eggs. It is likely this happened over and over until wisdom crept into our collective consciousness. How this applies to children needs to breach our consciousness. The more their identities include aspects of the world beyond their physical bodies, the greater their resilience.

When their rivers become deltas they are less vulnerable to a blockage in their flows.

Narrowness, lopsidedness, and rigidity all create vulnerability. The broader, more balanced, and more fluid their identity, the more stable and healthy they become. *I'm rubber, you're glue. What you say bounces off me and sticks to you.* This is another enduring schoolyard saying. Wonderfully insightful if we stop and reflect. Our objective is to create rubber children. Ones whose breadth, balance, and fluidity in the way they see themselves make them closer to being impervious to hurtful attacks. Insulation and shields are necessary for inner peace in a world of slings and arrows.

Serenity is not freedom from the storm but peace within the storm. This Native American proverb should encourage us to breathe. We spend much effort trying to create utopian life spaces for our young, free from conflict and pain. This is unrealistic. Life's nature is littered with conflict and pain. We can minimize this turbulence, but if the craft is not steady, even a small wind can topple it. Serenity is available to our little brothers and sisters in such doses that, if they swallow the full amount, they can remain standing in any storm.

Whole identity is one of these sources of serenity. It provides youth a wide base and therefore good balance and stability. A fragmented, narrow identity is a stool on one leg. That it remains upright at all should be a surprise. A child who sends her roots into all living things, gains the strength and balance of all living things. A great cloud of peace drifts over her, swallows her. She swallows it. With this tranquility inside, she barely hears the roar of life's waves crashing.

Her heart journal: *They don't know this yet. One day I'll shine. They'll stop and feel. I am the eternal sunrise. I am. I be. I will.*

ATTACHMENT AND BONDING

Attachment is a dynamic that exists along a continuum of degrees or intensity. Each of us, throughout life, experiences fluctuations in our degree of attachment in each of our relationships—a continual ebb and flow. Attachment changes our neurological and physiological settings. So does detachment. Both are trains of momentum carrying us further in the direction of that change. We should take advantage of signs of attachment in a child.

This is a delicate balancing act. We do not want to push too hard. But when she is moving in the direction of attachment, changes are occurring in her brain, heart, and nervous system. She is opening up, becoming physiologically available for bonding. In the midst of that opening, if we can introduce moments and elements that feel good to her, we can further the opening.

When we see signs of detachment, this is also a train of momentum picking up speed. The sooner we are able to bring this kind of change to a halt the easier the task. Detachment is not just an emotional withdrawal. It involves the clouding of a reflection pond. Perceptions change. Thoughts of retreat flood the mind: *This space is no longer safe. I no longer belong here. I need to find safety.* If we can provide safe spaces for a child, even if those spaces are not with us, she may come back to us as a secondary function of feeling safe. We should try to resist taking detachment personally. This can shut down our creativity and prevent us from imagining new safe spaces for her.

Each successive separation (trauma) leaves behind incremental wounds that blockade the avenues of a child's ability to receive and offer love. Just as plaque obstructs blood from flowing through arteries. Obstructed arteries bring us heart attack and stroke. Obstructed attachment channels (cognitive, behavioral, affective, spiritual, creative) bring her similar systemic breakdowns. These breakdowns manifest as injuries to her whole, creating further inflammation to her internal channels.

This is the circular trap of trauma. Trauma creates separation. Separation creates a wound. Wounding creates a need to protect that wound. The need to protect often manifests as a further drive toward separation. This is the psychological echo of past traumas and dysfunctions. In many ways, we are taught by this detaching world how to separate and detach. With practice, we become expert, as with anything else we repeat over and again.

We may repair certain detachment wounds in a youth's whole identity by strengthening other existing attachments. For example, writing clarifies her self-concept, which strengthens her capacity to feel connected to her heritage. Athletics increases her esteem, which strengthens her sense of worthiness to be loved. Growing back into her biological family strengthens her attachment to her expanded family. Strengthening her sense of femaleness increases the health of her bond with maleness.

Her social environments and all the relationships therein may be conceived of as a collective social unit, much like her family. Her ability to bond or attach within her social circle is paramount to her healthy development. Because of her inherent separation wounds or traumas, her development path may become vulnerable.

The landscape of her attachment striving is littered with fears and challenges, much like ours is. Her most persistent refrains: *Will I be liked and accepted? What are people's hidden prejudices about me? No one understands me.*

Past betrayals of her trust are flames that keep licking away, leaving her blistered. She is trying to be obedient to her authority figures even as she suffocates from a lack of voice. She is learning how to please but in doing so she is vulnerable to being used. She works to fit in as she obsesses over not standing out. Her fear of rejection mixes with her impermanent sense of relationships, creating a heart full of mortar, rigid and resistant to love.

Homework is handed out at home, too. Satisfying her parents' expectations is a chore that seems never to be completed. Calm is a fantasy. Her hummingbird heart, fluttering without pause, is trying to learn that failure is not catastrophic. It is so hard for her to believe that her imperfections will not incite further abuse, violence, or abandonment.

Until she learns that discipline is love, life will not make sense. But what strange language is this? The lines between discipline and the punishment that she knows too well are wisps of smoke. She has so many new roles to fulfill: child, sibling, student, explainer of her pain. The roles step on each other's feet and confuse her. She has been given a library of new traditions, rituals, and unspoken rules. We expect her to learn them quickly. But where are all the librarians to interpret the volumes?

She walks a high wire, a tension strung between independence and dependence. Her self-worth is a fragile sprout that grows in both soils. She needs privacy so she can work this out but her stigmatized life feels as though it is an open book. She feels her shameful pages are blowing out the window. Everybody is picking them up, reading them, whispering. Her whole world expects her to attach and bond in the middle of this tempestuous carnival. She wants to. In her wanting is a question: *If I join you in this intimacy, will you be my protection?*

How have others been our protectors? In our safest, most secure relationships, honesty and consistency were among the prized building materials. No deceptions, no sudden re-dealing of the cards. She is playing the same game we are.

DETACHMENT FLOWS

Children become more vulnerable to development challenges the more detachment they suffer. Two social factors are prominent triggers for detachment:

DISTANCE FROM NORMAL. The further any of a child's personal traits are from the social norm, the more vulnerable she becomes to the detachment wounds that can result. *Distance from the norm* increases her likelihood of vulnerability, but is not automatically a direct cause of her behavior or attitude. Any aspect of a child (heritage, language, physical or learning capacity, trauma, separation, social class, etc.) can cause her to fall prey to the hurtful tide of being related to as *abnormal*.

THE NUMBER OF "NON-NORMAL" TRAITS. The more traits a child carries that are nonstandard inside her social circles, the more vulnerable she is to suffering detachment wounds. These wounds can impact her learning experience, among many other factors. Again, these nonstandard traits create the likelihood of vulnerability. We can use this likelihood profile to prevent harm and to intervene on her behalf. Children should be treated with preventive and intervening strategies that focus on healing detachment wounds.

Another focus should be strengthening existing connections and relationships children have within their whole identity. For instance, a child dealing with a history of sexual abuse can be encouraged to develop her artistic inclinations, or her positive sense of being female. These strengthened aspects of her whole identity can then empower her to heal her sexual abuse trauma.

OUR CULTURE OF DETACHMENT

Our world is increasingly a culture of detachment. Flashing, exploding, racing audio and visual stimuli flood our days. Technology pours a hyper-excitement into our ears, eyes, and brains. Families are more fragmented than ever—physically and socially. Instead of concepts of family that stress expansion, we stress fractions: step-children and parents, half-siblings. This fractioned labeling has an effect on relationships that should be *whole*.

Our natural individual rhythms are disrupted by the pace of our collective living. Stress rises like a creeping tide, itself a detaching stimulus. Our children's education is largely doled out in parts, not as a whole integrated continuum. The need to standardize our evaluation of students feeds into this.

Our nutritional substance and habits detach us from our natural state of being—physiologically, emotionally, and mentally. Our foods are processed and polluted. We rush through our meals, overeat, and yet are malnourished.

Even creativity is oppressed in our overwhelmed race toward material security. We squeeze the arts, music, and physical activity out of our youths' lives. Creativity is a primal force for attachment and wholeness. It allows the self to flow into the whole and vice versa.

The effect of this expansive detachment is to create unsettledness in each of us. Our most vulnerable succumb in predictable ways. Asking detached children to exist within a detaching environment and yet become grounded and secure is a tall order. Reflecting on how we can bring calm and stillness to their lives is greatly helpful.

Detachment becomes generational. We should be concerned with how these children carry their attachment challenges into adulthood. They become the parents, extended family, educators, role models, healers, and child development professionals into which the next generations of traumatized children wade. We keep lighting more and bigger fires in the social forest our youth inhabit: fires of anger, anxiety, disconnection, cruelty, and an unnatural pace of living. Our youth feel the singe of these fires and jump more and higher. We scorn and criticize them for jumping. We demean and vilify them. We are a frustrated shepherd whose flock is running amok all over the mountain pass. But we set the fires from which they are running.

They are chameleons who take on the nature of the environment we create for them. Maybe we should take a moment to catch our breath, take inventory of our lives. Can we calm our own conflagration, provide them with a more docile air to breathe? Can we light fewer fires beneath their feet?

BEAUTY AND BELONGING

Beauty and belonging are fraternal twins tugging at each other's umbilicus. Each needs the other's nutrients. Neither can live without the other. Beauty defines herself through belonging—her sense of her place in the world. Belonging defines herself through beauty—how she shines in the world. Both of these dynamics are streams running through a child, depositing internal wealth or poverty according to their fullness.

A child's sense of belonging to all things—holistic connectedness—leads to positive growth, healing, and attitudes. Belonging fosters a critically important sense of beauty. Belonging is not a physical thing. Having a bedroom in a home does not create belonging if a child feels unsafe in that bedroom. And what does it matter if we have adopted, fostered, mentored, or sponsored a child if she does not feel her roots extending into our soil?

Belonging depends upon a child feeling as though she has a valuable purpose in the relationship. She must feel that the person with whom she belongs needs her, respects her, and honors where she has been as well as where she is going. As she feels *There is a reason I am here, with these people, in this community*, she is experiencing belongingness.

Youth often don't recognize that they are experiencing non-belonging. Their anxieties spill out all over the place. They can't tell us what they are feeling or why. We are lost in helping them. Beauty and belonging are always good places to start. If we explore these areas, youth may begin to offer clues as to the source of their suffering. We need to become skilled at recognizing the signs of children who do not feel they belong. We need to become familiar with the pangs of their non-beauty.

A child's sense of her beauty must be based in her appreciation of her nature, spirit, personality, intelligence, ability. Her sense of true beauty is not a satisfaction with cosmetic, bodily appearance. It is her feeling that she is worthy of love, respect, and honor: *I am a good person. I am valuable in this world. My whole being is attractive. I have something to offer people.* These are the thought patterns and affect of a child with a sense of authentic beauty.

Flowing water in the natural world can help us to understand the movement of beauty and belonging. We tend to overlook the nature of streams. These flowing gifts are not just water. They carry sediment and fertilizing matter downstream, bringing new life to depleted soil. We can continually create beauty streams in young lives.

Together, we compose evolving portraits of their gifts and purpose, carried downstream over time, through their seasons of change. This recalls the African serenades to the young girl at her meaningful life passages. When she goes through changes, she momentarily loses a grip on her confidence and worth. Beauty streams, in song and other celebration, are reminders that she is still priceless. Beauty streams are a way of calming her fears: *Hush little darling, everything's going to be all right. You're still beautiful in my sight.*

BALANCING BEAUTY

In our relationship with the world, two kinds of beauty consume us: common beauty and uncommon beauty. Common beauty is the beauty we share with others, a thing often bestowed by being a part of the norm, the mainstream, the prevailing inclination. Uncommon beauty is the part of our beauty that makes us stand out. It is the young girl who plays the violin so gracefully in a friendship circle of non-musicians; or the boy who speaks French in a small English-speaking town.

Every child has a unique balance point between these two needs. Children who are not only separated but culturally distinct, have their own sensitive balance point. This can affect their experience as they negotiate social conformity and personal allegiance.

Whether a child defines one of her traits as beautiful is a matter of both social opinion and personal opinion. Of course the two are so intertwined they nearly merge. Especially in children deplete of familial and other reflection ponds.

We help a child strike her balance points by allowing her to dictate when, how often, and how much she wishes her common and uncommon beauty to be highlighted. The same is true for her stigmatized experiences and traits. School, home, and community are all theatres for her beauty and shame to be played out. She is a capable playwright, director, and actor. Working ourselves respectfully into the cast, we are best positioned to assist in the balancing of her beauty.

This can be a delicate dance. Care is necessary in not making her feel like a poster child for her separation experience. Our running away from what she feels is shameful about her, leaves her feeling that we too view that part of her as shameful. Learning her balance points comes with compassionate listening, an act that involves our heart more than our ears.

Children need to balance their beauty in another way as well. As long as their sense of physical, emotional, mental, and spiritual beauty is not in balance, they will walk wobbling on their paths. Nothing out of balance moves or operates gracefully. There is always ungainliness. This kind of comprehensive system imbalance produces a sensation of intoxication—the child feels out of control. Her vision is distorted. She has daily hangovers from all the wobbling. Balancing this beauty is an urgent task.

Balancing her beauty within the web of her wholeness is also an important objective. If her sense of beauty resides predominantly in only one aspect of herself, such as her body, she will focus inordinately on that aspect. She will call undue social attention to her body. She will hang out the shingle of her body to attract the world toward the one thing she truly believes is beautiful about her.

This lopsided self-perception of her beauty creates more wobbling, like a tottering gyroscope. Notice how the balanced gyroscope spins longer? A child with a sense of beauty spread evenly through her wholeness moves more efficiently as well. She moves more fluidly, gracefully, effectively through her life.

LATE TO THE PARTY

Have you ever arrived late to a party and felt as if everyone else was already in on something you missed? They seemed to be in a conversation and rhythm that you could not join or catch up on. With each moment your discomfort grew, your anxieties rose. You became self-conscious and began to feel as if you did not belong, all because you arrived late to the party. Even your esteem was affected. You felt less attractive, less likeable, almost rejected and devalued.

Ultimately, you decided to leave early or you stayed but never quite felt right. This scenario is very similar to the experience of many uprooted children. To us, everything may seem in place for their positive experience with new family, school, and community. But for the children, this is a party that everyone else has arrived at first. Uprooted children are late to the scene. This by itself can cause them to feel like misfits. Being aware of this can increase our understanding and helpfulness.

Many separated children experience the phenomenon of perpetual flying. This is a dream state in which they feel as though they never have a place to land. They are forced to remain aloft. Their wings grow exhausted. A slow surrender seeps into them as they begin to believe they can't stay aloft any longer. The horror of this dream state is that many youth experience it during their every waking hour.

Do you remember occasions when you were the only one present who wasn't speaking a certain language unfamiliar to you? Do you recall feeling left out of the conversation? Maybe feelings of inadequacy arose, or suspicion that you were being talked about. You may have simply felt as though you were on the outside looking in. Whatever the feeling, it is likely that you did not feel good. This is how children can feel when they enter a family, classroom, or community from an outside source. They feel as though everyone is speaking the same language except them. The culture discrepancy can feel like a wall. Their outsider identity becomes magnified.

We may feel the same way in relation to these youth as they enact a way of being that seems foreign to us. As they grow older and develop social circles that perpetuate that foreign way of being, we grow more threatened by our outsider status. There is a way out of this for both us and youth. We can learn to speak the same language.

Honoring children's heritage creates a shared language between us. The more we honor and discover youths' heritage the more we acquire a common language. This is a powerful bridge for bonding, trust, and safety. It does not cost us anything to be humble and learn where a child is coming from, figuratively and otherwise. The payoff is large. No one feels good being left out of the conversation.

PUPPET SHOW

So much of the way a child acts, reacts, thinks, and feels is a puppet show. Her strings are being pulled by her past experiences. Also controlling her marionette-state are her fearful projections of the future. Cutting all these strings and beginning to exist according to her nature and purpose can be a lifelong project.

Her process of un-becoming a puppet depends on access to evidence that she is a real human being. This may seem nonsensical. But the struggle of many adults, not to mention children, is that they exist never fully present in the world. Never completely believing they are real, they live life as if it is a relentless dream.

A child's introductions to her essence come through a cycle of creativity, sharing, receiving, and validation. She needs hundreds of these cycles whirling within each of her days. She was born to sing, wired to be heard. She is song and she is bird. Creativity cycles force her to feel. Deep emotional sensation is like a familiar voice pulling her out of a dream, or a hand pulling her up from beneath her drowning water.

The more she encounters her feelings, the more evidence she accumulates that she is real. The more consistently she acts according to her true nature. Success from her true nature further feeds her healing and transformation. The puppet nature inside her dies only when she encounters a substitute nature she can trust. Her challenge is to fall in love with her true nature. The two of them need sweet time together.

MIMIC MASTERS

Children who desperately seek out their beauty by siphoning it from others become mimic masters. They will try on everyone's *clothing* but their own. If they stand out, they will do everything in their power to erase what makes them stand out and adopt the appearance and ways of those around them. They put on the costume of the dominant social groups or individuals in their lives. We might think of this as a cute evolution of children toward a way of being we are comfortable with. We are deceived.

When children mimic the beauty of others, they are swimming upstream. This introduces a resistance to their life. Daily existence becomes more of an effort because they are going against their natural grain. Just as when we move our hand against the grain of wood, their life becomes a board of splinters. They suffer pangs and needles where they would not if only they could be encouraged to turn in their own intended direction.

MIND IS A HEART-KEY

The mind is a key the heart has been given to unlock the door of two homes. One home is a sanctuary where all the heart's desires are fulfilled. The heart's tender spots are massaged by magical hands. The heart soaks in a tub of tranquility and joy. Stress and fear can hardly enter this house. Its very nature repels such energy.

In this sanctuary every wound the heart incurs is well healed in time. The windows let in fresh restorative air. Each room is filled with curing drafts. The walls are compassionate, the mirrors reveal only beauty. Revelation grows in the darkness of the closets. The basement hums with truth. The flooring is solid and secure, the roof and ceiling powerfully protective. This place is possible in young lives.

The other home is where despair holds a daily chorus.

These are two very different perceptual homes. Both dwellings shape our entire existence. Don't we wish our beloved young will choose their residence wisely? A good locksmith fashions keys to a polished fit. Our children have given us a challenging job. Whatever our station in life, we have been made honorary locksmiths to assist their habitation. Let's shape good keys.

NATURAL SCIENCE OF CHANGE

The mind is our tool for change. The heart is our fuel for change. The body observes the rules of change. Understanding this relationship is the art of change.

The human mind is much more similar in nature to our muscles than we may realize. Thoughts exist as electrical impulses racing from neuron to neuron in the brain. Changing thought patterns from negative to positive, from small self to big self, is a matter of changing the highways over which we direct our thought traffic.

We may need to install signs for warning, yielding, or detours. These signs are the mental exercises in which we engage. After enough repetition, just as with our muscles, the mind becomes trained to think in certain ways, to generate certain feelings. We will still need to exercise the right thought patterns to keep the highway clear and avoid going off-course, but the habit will have been set.

Our mind is so similar to and synched with our muscles that thought actually *is* behavior. Thought generates electrical activity that fires the nerves in our muscles. Every thought has a corresponding physical response. Angry thoughts literally clench our heart and constrict our blood vessels. Loving thoughts physically relax and open our heart and vessels. Even in our dreams, which we think of as a mental landscape, every dream image creates a reaction in our body.

This is how visualization works. We mentally take our body through dress rehearsals. Our muscles and nervous system act out or simulate their anticipated behavioral roles. Thought *is* behavior. This means that thought exercises are actually behavioral exercises. A child's behavior changes as her thoughts change. She needs a mental workout.

Just as with her muscles, to strengthen thought processes, her neurons need to experience resistance with each repetition. This resistance is the effort of change. It does not come easily. Our children need to become aware that they are just as capable of transforming their low self-esteem into high self-regard as they are of developing their athletic or musical skills. All such change requires practice—resistance and repetition.

A virtually mathematical dynamic to mental change exists: resistance (thought) x repetition = change. Our neurons become more efficient at thinking positively each time we think positively. These neurons also increase in number to handle the workload as we exercise them in a particular way. Our muscles grow in the same way. The fibers become stronger, more efficient, and greater in number as we expose them over and again to exercise tasks. This is the science of the mind. Healing and transformation are not mystical or magical. They are practical and mundane. We have been hard-wired to change in response to the right stimuli.

This interplay of stimulus and response is on display all around us in nature. The movements are not called exercise or practice but force, friction, and time. The forces of gravity, heat, cold, wind, water, and fire create friction and pressure. Friction and pressure exerted repeatedly over time result in transformation. For our children, we can liken their life challenges to the transformation that turns earth into diamonds, rubies, coral, and pearls. And to the forces that metamorphose caterpillar into butterfly and one season into the next.

Nothing in nature is born without struggle. A healthy child too will be born through struggle. She will be born into happiness, peace, lightness of being. She will be born into confidence, faith, and purpose. We have our own birthing stories to offer her, to show her how change is birth and becoming; that change is dying and letting go. Just as the snake struggles to shed its many skins, we humans must endure effort and discomfort, and even pain, as we graduate moment by moment into our true selves.

A child depends on us to teach her that this cycle of struggle and becoming is undeniably normal, natural. We can point out the parade of struggle-born change being conducted all around her, every day. From this she can begin to develop eyes for seeing change and a heart that surrenders to the beauty of struggle. River struggles to become a waterfall. Waterfall struggles to become a river again. This is living. As she sees this truth, the web of life is revealed and she realizes she is not alone.

Through our persistent, patient sharing, we normalize loss, trauma, healing, and growth cycles as functions of a natural unfolding. We transform youths' traumatized, negative concept of change into the blessing of change. We repeat our drumbeat: *With each change comes an opportunity to fade or grow; to know yourself better; reveal yourself. This is how you become grown and powerful.*

In the same way, we can transform the concept of past change as involving relationship termination or disruption. Our young can learn to associate current and future change as involving relationship permanency and strengthened bonds.

Another lesson we can pull out of our life drawer is that of re-anchoring within each change. We can teach the skills we have acquired for achieving identity clarity, esteem, and worth in the midst and aftermath of change.

We have learned how to evaluate relationships as we change, and to discern which relationships belong in our lives. Someone has to teach our young these skills. This is not a part of their basic school curriculum. But it will determine the heft of their happiness to a greater degree than any coursework.

When children mentor other children who are going through a similar change, the mentor is strengthened. Where are our programs for engaging transitional youth in being mentors? We can create simple opportunities within our own families and schools. Teaching change endurance is the best way to learn to endure change.

Whole identity is an anchor for positive reactions to change. This way of seeing self creates internal security and stability independent of external factors and change. It provides a buffer or insulation against the traumatic side effects of change. It is a sweet reminder of self in the storm or in the cacophony of group persuasion. Wholeness helps resist negative peer pressure. Seeing life narrowly, change can horrify. Seeing life broadly, change becomes a friend. Sometimes that friend shows up uninvited, unannounced. In the house of a child's wholeness, she is prepared to receive her unpredictable friend.

Human attitudes and behavior drift toward the average. There are collective and personal averages. Children tend to gravitate toward the average behavior in a group. They tend to gravitate toward their own average behavior. Average and conformity: spinning sameness exerting a gravitational pull. Mediocrity is a force of gravity. To change attitudes and behaviors, new personal and collective averages can be created, and work can be done to resist regression toward harmful averages.

In many ways the two strategies are the same. When children change their personal averages in a healthy direction they become more resistant toward the pull of harmful social group averages. They are less tethered to negative conformity. We may find it easier to encourage new groups into young lives, thereby changing the average group behavior to which youth are exposed. Regardless of the approach, changing average behavior and attitudes with a child or group requires exposure to new stimuli, and thought and behavior patterns. Activating wholeness in one or many children creates a drift toward healthier average behavior and attitudes.

Individually and collectively, we adults have much changing of our own to do. As we acquire these change skills we can pass them on to youth. Changing norms or ways of being requires courage and a sense of self-relevance to the work of change. It requires committed, clear, visionary leadership and immediacy (a sense of crisis). And the person changing must believe she can change. This is one of the most essential ingredients.

Opportunity to exercise the habits of change is crucial, as is role clarity within the process of change. There should be meaningful consequences to both positive change and negative behavior. Change should be celebrated as it is incrementally achieved. We benefit by promoting the effort toward change. This creates broader social awareness, resulting in support and commitment.

We should project timely outcomes for our change efforts. Evidence of the work always does the heart good. Open channels for feedback and communication are vital, even when the change project is only a personal one. Even then we need to be in communication with ourselves about the experience. Taking inventory of our feelings, thoughts, challenges, and insights fuels our progress.

We need to monitor our self-knowledge and identity as they transform within the change process. Creative self-expression can aid this. Awareness of who we are can slip away from us in the midst of change. Creating space and opportunity for healing during change is valuable. With change comes both letting go and birthing. Both processes involve a need to heal. Tapping into our whole identity anchors us through the journey. Change brings turbulence.

The more strands we hold onto, the more of our internal rivers we replenish from, the greater our ability to ride out the transformation.

OUR SELF-SERVING NATURE

Our nature as human beings is to be persistently motivated by self-interest. This is largely a survival instinct, though also very much a product of socialization. The history of social and personal change shows us that appealing to self-interest is much more likely to produce change than appealing to morals. This is true for us and for our young. It is imperative that we create clear, compelling arguments for child-honoring attitudes and behavior—in youth and in ourselves. The personal consequences of not doing so must be made painfully clear, along with the concrete benefits of such growth.

If our own house is on fire we will act to put out the fire much more quickly than if a neighbor's house is on fire. When a child is in crisis, we all need to believe that our own house is on fire. Honoring a child's heritage, including her story, is not a matter of morality but a matter of practicality and our own survival. To the degree we understand her, we uplift her. Her vitality feeds ours.

Whole identities dispel the fragmenting *us vs. them* mentality our society embeds within us. Self-interest grows into our perception of other people's lives. We realize that we truly rise and fall together. Such ways of seeing create true connectedness between individuals and groups. In this state of relating to one another, the troubles of children become our priorities. Together we inherit the wind of social well-being.

CREATING HEALTHY SOCIAL HABITS

We enlarge or reduce others in our own eyes based on our perceptual habits. We reduce and enlarge ourselves through the same habits. Enlargement is the act of imagining the beautiful whole within a person. Reduction imagines the person as a flawed fragment, neglecting to see her other aspects.

Children develop their own personal habits for how they relate to others. The habits range from constructing people to destructing people. When youth habitually construct people they are motivated to see their beauty, to be compassionate, and to be a positive presence in their lives. This occurs whether youth are interacting with others or just thinking about them.

Habitual destruction involves perceiving people's flaws and inferiority, judging and criticizing them, and being a hurtful presence in their lives. Children have the power to make choices about which habit they adopt. We need to be very present in encouraging them to adopt constructive relational habits.

Both habits involve initiating factors and secondary factors. Initiating factors are those traits of others that trigger secondary factors: emotions and thoughts. Initiating factors include traits that make people unique or similar, in both positive and negative ways. Virtually any trait can be an initiating factor. If a child is motivated to see beauty in others he will see it in any imaginable trait, including ones that others judge as negative.

Secondary factors—the thoughts and emotions arising from the initial triggers—include jealousy, threat, appreciation, gratitude, etc. Any thought or feeling can be a secondary factor. When the links between others' traits and our resulting thoughts and emotions become strong enough, an association has been created. This is the basis for mental schemas (pictures we fit people into based upon traits) and prejudice. Prejudice is part of a destructive habit. Other schemas can be positive. This is how a constructive child sees beauty in everyone—by developing a strong positive association with many of the traits people carry. He has learned to dig deep to find beauty.

We aid youth when we work with them to develop reasons for thinking and feeling positively about others. A strong motivator for this is self-interest. Can we find ways to convince youth that the well-being of others is in their own self-interest? Can we show them how compassion, affection, and generosity enrich their own life? If we can tell them this story of reciprocity regularly, it encourages their motivation to develop people-constructing habits. Children who have experienced rupture and isolation can use all the socially constructive energy they can gather.

Youth also need us to teach them creative ways of de-escalating the frequent conflicts of their social life. Our own life is our syllabus. We have many examples and insights to offer that can empower them to identify the consequences of conflict and its resolution. They need to learn the mental skill for doing a quick personal cost-benefit analysis of the two paths. We can equally empower them to identify the processes involved in conflict and resolution. Creating constructive habits in children is not enough. We need to also create these life affirming habits in the systems that touch their lives.

INSTITUTIONAL CHANGE

We often use backward approaches in attempting to create institutional change, in families or other systems. When the objective is to create *cultural competency* and *to honor diversity* we need to take care. Such rhetorical phrases become meaningless without investment in the appropriate courses of action. We cannot realistically expect institutional climate changes if we have not laid the building blocks for honoring heritage and culture.

A foundation is a necessary first step in constructing solid change. If we are creating a space that honors heritage, we have to create a thoughtful process that will clarify how we have failed to honor heritage in the first place. The process should clarify what it means to honor heritage. It should involve as authority the voices of those who feel as though their heritage has not been honored.

The idea that honoring heritage is a charitable act of benevolence to *special* others has to be exorcised from systemic cultures. Honoring culture as a positive, self-serving concept needs to be internalized individually and institutionalized. Commitment to this change should be strongest at the highest levels of leadership. No tolerance should be given to individual violations of the new values.

In business, workers are very motivated to be clear on what will cost them their jobs and what they can get away with. If they feel their job depends on making certain personal changes, they are malleable. When institutions claim they have tried to make change but have met with resistance, they have not fully tried. They have not created an imperative in the minds of workers. Preserving the integrity of children who pass through our families and systems should not be something *being worked on*. It should be a crisis-oriented, leadership-demanded revolution.

CHILD-CENTERED SOCIETY

Powerful forces agitate on behalf of adults who want children and for institutions that profit from children. Who agitates for the rights of children? Who risks all to demand for the young access to their past, their origins, their honor, and their truth? A compassionate society generates its own endless waves of revolutionaries. Nonconformists daring to conceive of a world in which the challenging needs of youth are paramount. Even as those needs conflict with adult agendas. To speak of children earns applause. To truly stand for children is to risk adult rebuke. Here is our place of reckoning.

Our children's direct voices should be increasingly interjected into law, policy, practice, parenting, and public life—on all matters pertinent to them. Failing to achieve this integration is demeaning and self-defeating. This is like creating temple or church support groups without receiving input from the congregants. Societal maturity is evident when the testimony of those who live an experience is treated as authoritative of that experience.

Legally possessing children is not the ultimate goal of a compassionate society. Healing and empowering the disrupted source from which children flow is the ultimate goal of a compassionate society. A compassionate society does not write laws exclusively to protect access for adults who want children. It creates laws that change the conditions at the root of child and family upheaval.

True child welfare writes laws first and foremost that emanate from the stories children tell of their experience as they grow toward being women and men. It writes laws that protect the rights of children to be placed in the care of adults who will not harm them. Abuse has many names. We hover vigilantly over the obvious abuses to body and physical neglect. So many more children are scalded and neglected each day by adults who fail to see them; adults who are afraid of them; adults who steamroll their own culture over the nubile stalk that is the child's culture. A compassionate society begins its work with the child's story and constructs a way home from there.

Our systemic approach to children tends to be case-oriented and focused on the individual. A child's case is considered either open or closed. The objective with an open case is to close it. But a child's life and her relationships are not cases to be closed. They are fluid realities forever open. Her life is a never-ending stream that runs through and beyond even her seasons of adulthood. It flows into successive generations. Her life is an unfinished truth. It requires continual learning, understanding, maintenance, and investment on the part of every person and institution involved. A fluid approach that considers her as though she is an extension of a generational social circle will serve us well.

His heart journal: *Who writes the law that says anyone who wants me can have me? I want a law that says anyone who has me has to want me. ALL OF ME.*

BEAUTY OUT OF CONTEXT

Children are unique prisms reflecting the light of the world so that it shines in new and useful ways. They shine in ways that only their uniqueness will allow. Shade their light and we kill the lantern they are meant to be. This is not poetry. It is hard truth.

Einstein must have been ridiculed mercilessly as a child. We only understand his beauty in the context of his later scientific creations. Martin Luther King, Jr. was likely criticized as a boy for being too sensitive and deep thinking. Only as a man were his traits widely recognized as gifts. Mother Theresa, when she was little, must have been admonished for caring too much. Gandhi was viewed as too serious a boy; Harriet Tubman, as too uppity a slave girl. And can we imagine the tongue lashings young Jesus, Moses, Muhammad, Buddha, and Krishna received for daring to not be like other children?

Because many of our children have been separated from their roots and have not yet achieved their purpose, they are at risk of being judged out of context. What makes them difficult, challenging, sullen, resistant, angry, or *mentally slow* in our eyes may in fact be their brilliance beginning to broil.

Members of their original families may have had similar traits. Knowing this would help us see the children clearer and be less judgmental. That backdrop is often not available to us. Yet, if we stretch ourselves beyond our habitual way of seeing, we can glimpse the positive meaning of their traits. This stretching is our responsibility, not theirs. We continue indirectly asking youth to explain their strangeness to us. They may only be strange in relation to us. Our similarity to others does not make us a more valid form of beautiful. We just happen to have more people available to recognize our beauty.

A mathematical genius in a family of athletes may feel like a loser, especially if her family ridicules her lack of athleticism and her cerebral ways. One day she is awarded the Nobel Prize. Now everyone has seen her beauty. How many of our young do we force to wait a lifetime to be celebrated? We have work to do. Our easy assumptions and judgments need to be suspended so that we are able to detect children's true value.

Just because we are surrounded by people who look, act, or think like us does not mean our way of being is superior to distinctive children. It might mean just the opposite. Our normalcy might simply be the consequence of our participation in conformity.

The small crystal heart on the table may seem empty and fairly meaningless until we place it on the windowsill where it becomes filled with light. Let us put our children in position so that their natural light shines through. When a child comes into our life who sees things in a way that is new to us, this is cause for a celebration. New gifts are about to be opened.

IDENTIFYING A CHILD'S PURPOSE

Purpose represents a child's most natural, intended avenues through which to share his light with the world. When anyone in a child's circle, including the child, misidentifies the child's gifts, a judgmental wind blows many of his reflection ponds away. Who knows whether a sensitive, deep feeling child will find his true life purpose in working with autistic children? He might not ever approach that path if he receives frequent criticism throughout childhood for being sensitive.

Instead of criticizing a young man for taking apart every electronic item in the house, we can recognize this as a sign of his gifts, his beauty. We can provide him the space and context for taking things apart and putting them back together. Now we have created a reflection pond of ourselves. He sees us as people who have embraced a passionate part of who he is. He sees that he grows in us.

Children especially tend to be criticized for what in fact is their gift when they find themselves in secondary families or new settings. This happens particularly when most of the new group members share a similar personality or nature distinct from the children's.

In our families and classrooms it is good to take inventory of the currents that define normalcy in those settings. Doing so, we become aware of the boundary between what traits are being validated and what are not. Once aware, we can stroke a distinctive child to his own sense of goodness. We should consistently teach people in a child's life space about the value of the child's underrated traits. This requires our appraisal of group norms and of the child's distinctiveness. What a wonderful investment in protecting him. He will drape blue ribbons of appreciation around our necks in his heart, where his truest ceremonies take place.

CREATIVE EXERCISES

We can create as many exercises as we wish to help a child tell us who he is. We can ask him to show us in writing or drawings his idea of the *Perfect Me* and the *Real Me*; his *Perfect World* and his *Real World*; his *Perfect Family* and his *Real Family*. What he creates in response tells us much about how he sees himself, us, and the world.

The world is a constant barrage of messages that wish to define a child. At no point does he lose the need to remind himself who he is and who he wishes to be. This should be a lifelong written or mental exercise. If he does not habitually complete the thought I AM—, the world will fill in the blanks. If he does not repeatedly clarify his ideal self, external forces will cause a seepage that fills him with their own foreign idea of who he should be.

We can ask him to write a story or draw a picture revealing what he could do if given the power to change the world. We allow him to imagine: *If I could change the world.* His rendering shows us what he cares about, what his values are, what he feels is wrong in his life and the lives of others. A similar effect is produced by the *I Wish* letters that he writes about what he wishes for, what he wishes were different, what he wishes he could do or be.

One value of exercises like this is that they speak directly to personal values. They locate a child's heart and mind for us, and for him, on the map of well-being.

A child has a natural curiosity. We can make him feel important and send him on a valuable quest to harvest the stories of his elders. This generational story harvesting enriches his sense of the world, reveals how the past is alive in him, and connects him to the elders he dearly needs in his life.

At any time, without much cost, we can invite a child to paint, dance, sing, act his emotions. He is a creative force waiting to be unleashed. He will come up with ways to portray his feelings that we would not imagine. Once portrayed, his emotions are available for self-discovery.

Here is my Heart exercises allow him to express what is in his heart in ways that feel safe. Along with journaling, such activities provide him with privacy, control, unrushed time, and internal focus. The creativity gets him in touch with himself.

Beyond his physical relationship with original family, he can enjoy a psychological and emotional relationship through writing. With our encouragement, he can write letters that he may or may not send to his original family, old friends, past community, and to his ancestry. He can write letters to his past self and to imagined descendants.

His letters can be his platform for updates, questions, grievance, sorrow, fantasy, humor. More than anything, they are exercises in connecting with his intimate social web. Through these writings, his mind, body, heart, and spirit are synchronized.

CREATIVE SELF-EXPRESSION

What children love will open them enough for truth to get in and out. If they love music, let them play their music as they express themselves. Let them express their story as music. They relax in the presence of what feels good to them. Have we spent enough energy learning what those things are? We can surround them with their passions, increasing the chance that they will open up. In our chaotic world and their uncertain lives, they greatly lack moments in which they simply feel good inside.

Creative self-expression can be a powerful medium for activating a healing process and bolstering esteem. Creativity flushes toxicity from the system and restores natural flow. Sports, science, music, writing, drawing, dancing, acting, journalism, debate, and leadership are among the almost endless ways children can creatively express themselves.

The way we engage youth in these processes can either dampen or perpetuate their interest and creativity. Whatever children produce, we should make sure to read, listen to, or watch, as long as they wish. Even better, we can write, sing, and produce along with them. We should let this creativity be relevant to what they care about. This is their cultural bonanza. We are the adoring guests.

It is important that we build reward factors into children's activities. Material rewards such as money and clothing may be obvious to us, but educational or nurturing rewards are all the better. Books, tickets to enlightening movies, museums, and music performances— all are material rewards with underlying growth value.

We can be creative and think of social, spiritual, and emotional rewards. Anything that brings positive attention to a child's creativity is a social reward. Publishing a child's creative work in the family, school, or community has great social impact on her. Publishing is the act of putting the creative work on display. She should be involved in any decisions about how her creativity will be displayed. Her sense of ownership over the entire process is a significant part of healing and empowerment. Seeing her poetry or paintings decorating the walls of her dentist's office is a powerful social reward. It creates buzz—verbalized compliments she receives directly or indirectly. Many of our children rarely get to enjoy being the subject of good buzz. When a child sees her essay published in the town paper and hears people talking about her writing, she is soaking up a social reward.

Any healthy reward or incentive has a spiritual and emotional benefit to it. It leaves children feeling good about themselves and activates pride and satisfaction. These kinds of rewards also may produce feelings of relief, cleansing, or healing. A child's creative action is the strongest spiritual and emotional reward. We simply need to help her recognize how she has rewarded herself through her creativity. Ask her: *How are you feeling having created this? Do you feel better having gotten it out of you?* She relies upon us to help her see the benefits of her creativity. Our feedback is as essential to her as the creativity itself.

This feedback should always be productive, constructive, and uplifting. Children often interpret feedback in a very sensitive manner. What we might feel is constructive, they may receive as criticism. When we are discussing with them how they might grow with their creativity, it helps if we couch our comments in a positive, complimenting light.

Sometimes a young man is expressing something creatively about delicate parts of his life. This is his story and no one has the right to own it other than him. When we allow him the choice of anonymity with his creativity, this may make him feel safer to create again. The power to have privacy while creating is a fundamental motivator. One of his great fears is that someone will take advantage of what he has expressed or done and use it to ridicule, hurt, or criticize him. It is very likely he has had this happen several times already. Our awareness of this feeds into the safe space he needs to inhabit for creativity.

When we witness in him signs that he has a talent or interest in a creative endeavor, this is the time for us to jump forward generously. Let us provide as many appropriate creative opportunities and platforms for him as we can without making him feel it is being forced on him. His fire might be lit further by developing relationships with those he admires who are involved in similar kinds of creativity. Now we are building a circle around him. He cannot have too many feel-good circles, groups in which he feels he belongs according to his song.

As he develops these creative circles, we can begin to create positive social status for him and his creative circle. We create social status by being creative about celebrating the beauty that his circle is producing. We promote, publish, create platforms, invite family and others to watch, learn, listen, behold. See how our creativity toward him feeds into his creativity about himself? This life is a gorgeous dream waiting for us to paint it in colors.

Let our imagination run wild. We can use community personalities as judges for poetry, singing, and dancing contests. Now we are creating community even as we are nurturing the creative child. As part of this vitality we should work with children to produce decency and safety guidelines for their creativity. There are so many age-appropriate ways our children can discover themselves beyond their often mundane daily routines.

Although children need and respond well to the right amount of order, they are not designed to be robotic. They are designed to create. When they are depressed and depleted of vitality it is not because vitality is not in them. It is because their creative vessels are gummed up and blocked. Woundedness has this effect. Our task is to help them open up the vessels. Their natural flow will do the rest. This is how healing gets made.

LETTER OF RESIGNATION

A young girl is desperate to feel good inside. Her heart literally is dying for some peace. Try as she might, she has been unable to unshackle herself from revolving thoughts of negativity and gloom. This incarceration inside the walls of despair is dire. She may be more motivated to climb out of this hole than we perceive. All she lacks is a ladder or some rope. Have her sit down and write a letter of resignation to her suffering. Her language will be unique to her personality and growth, but here is a mature example of the ideas her letter can contain:

I hereby resign from this place of anger and fear. My time here has been very unhealthy for me. I have decided to move into a new occupation. Its name is Peace. It offers wonderful benefits, such as happiness, healing, laughter, friendship, and fulfillment. Parking is free—I can stay there as long as I want without charge. The work involves great travel opportunities. Destinations are global and include Discovery, Epiphany, Revelation, and Becoming. Tourist safety has always been rated among the highest in those countries.

I do not regret my time here. Although it has often been difficult, I realize that I can take many lessons from my experiences. My suffering and pain are now part of my résumé; I can use them as reminders of what it feels like to not work and live at a place like Peace. In my new life I look forward to advancing and growing on a daily basis.

Eventually I will own the company. No one will ever be able to fire me. I will always own my Peace. Thank you again for this opportunity. I wish you well in the future and leave you on good terms. Please feel free to visit me periodically in Peace, for I realize that you, Suffering, are a part of Peace. But with all due respect, please understand that you will not be allowed to stay long. That's just how it is with Peace.

She can write an actual resignation letter like this, in words or in pictures. The level of sophistication is not vital. All that matters is that she engages her mind, her body, and her heart in the act of consciously resigning from her entrapment with suffering. Suffering has a lease we often outstay. It can serve a purpose in deepening our peace, but only when we know when to leave its house and go home. Peace is that home.

She can write this letter once a week, every month, or daily. The more often she writes the letter and meditates on what she has written, the more she enacts a systematic departure from her negative rut. Mind, heart, and muscle have conspired to see her free. In the same spirit she can write letters of acceptance. In those letters she can speak directly to Peace and Happiness, asserting her embrace of health and well-being. To top it all off, we can write our own letter along with her as she writes hers. This ritual can be our shared healing and a written trek toward one-on-one intimacy.

DECLARATION OF INTERDEPENDENCE

As our youth surge toward their imagined independence we would do well to remind them of this inescapable truth: *Everything I want in life I have to go through relationships to get.* There is no escaping the web. Independence is a function of grasping *inter*dependence. Becoming a good husband, wife, parent, sibling, teacher, leader, proprietor, citizen—all require being able to operate within the context of relationships. Obtaining a job and keeping a job—both require managing relationships.

We can teach an adolescent all the life skills we wish. If she is not capable of existing in a healthy way within relationships, those life skills will be wasted. Life skills cannot be translated into a skillful life without the necessary internal work and healing. If she does not believe she has a niche or purpose to apply the skills we teach her, those skills cannot take root in her active life.

A college-educated young man filled with anger and despair has the skills for independence yet lacks the capacity for interdependence. He is an explosion waiting to happen. Even worse, his condition is contagious to his peers. Despair travels in waves and reaches us all.

Youth must be taught how to manage their anger, disappointment, pain, and *failure*; even as we celebrate their successes. If they do not understand the sacrifice and loyalty involved in friendship, or the respect involved in honoring a loved one, how can they achieve togetherness?

A single relationship is at the crux of interdependence and life satisfaction: a relationship with the self. This is a critical doorway into youths' relationship with their whole. A relationship with self does not just happen, especially in alienating cultures in which youth drift away from themselves like silken strands from the web.

A relationship with self is a particular challenge on the after-side of trauma, which has such a self-detaching effect. Under such circumstances youth have to be taught the skills for acquiring a relationship with self. Reflection, meditation, creative self-expression—all are mechanisms for discovering and embracing self. The mechanisms need to be practiced.

To extend beyond a relationship with the small self out into a relationship with the big self, the collective whole, the same mechanisms are useful. Practice needs to be devoted. Resistance and repetition are the formula for creating whole identity and self-affirming thoughts and behavior. Resistance is the force of effort. These new thoughts about self and the world do not come easily and do not sink in readily. There will be resistance. Effort will be necessary to overcome that resistance.

Repetition of the thoughts involved with a healthy, clear identity is fundamental to growth. This consistent, daily practice is encouraged when youth have safe spaces in which to practice, when they are mentored or coached in practicing, and when practice is rewarded.

The more individualistic the world becomes, the more youth may find their peace and well-being through interdependence. Documents such as the *Declaration of Independence* have become potent forces, helping to establish mindsets of individualism. Each child has a healthy balance point between individualism and collectivism or between the small self and the larger self.

To aid against alienation, isolation, and despair, we can have our youth create their own potent documents for change. They can author personal *Declarations of Interdependence* and post them in the homes, lockers, and Internet spaces of their lives. The declarations can be written and audio- and video-recorded. These creative documents assert youths' right to access relationships that honor who they are, relationships that contain the elements they feel are important. The declarations can be reminders to youth of the importance of compassion, forgiveness, respect, and communication. Their families, classrooms, teams, and social groups can also create shared declarations of interdependence that facilitate bonds. National documents written hundreds of years ago have a strong effect on our group and personal identities today. We can use the power of declarations to change identities and prepare youth to participate in the vital relationships of their lives.

Depending upon our state of being, life is either an invisible web we trounce through recklessly with our thought, emotion, and behavior, or it is an intricate weaving revealed in the sunlight. When the web is revealed, and when it dawns in us that we are a most vulnerable strand suspended within that silken weaving, we shudder into self-recognition. Everything changes. We become caretakers of others and of the world. We begin to learn how peace is made and where beauty grows.

A STORY OF BELONGING

The young girl desperately seeks out people with whom she belongs. Her desperation makes her exaggerate and force herself. Those on the receiving end are repelled. It does not feel good having someone trying too hard or forcing themselves on you. The girl may belong just fine with certain people and groups. She will never know. Her urgent drive creates rejection she takes as yet more evidence of her inferiority.

Her anxieties rise. Her esteem plummets. She needs to belong, and to know with whom she belongs. She is holding her breath until she gets there. People are uneasy around girls holding their breath. They need her to breathe so they can breathe. Tension breeds tension. She cannot win. The more alienated she feels the more she holds her breath. She is looking for stamps of approval by banging too hard on too many doors. Her anger at not belonging needs some place to go. She swells with pressure.

Is this your child? If so, her acceptance into groups is not the first step. The first step is her letting go of her breath. We cannot diminish her need for acceptance. But we can work on improving her esteem. We can point out the ways in which she is already accepted, not just by her family but by every part of her whole.

Her sense of belonging is self-perpetuating. Her downward cycle creates more aversion in others. But as she fills out her whole she becomes less anxious and needy. Others are more attracted to her. They do not sense desperation. Ironically, as she begins to shine, and people flock to her light, she realizes that she does not need to belong everywhere and that she cannot please everyone. In that moment she is illuminated by many degrees, and becomes imminently more attractive.

Ideally, she comes to a place where she seeks only belonging with herself. She knocks on her inner doors that open up to new self-discoveries. This takes care of her social belonging. She is anchored internally. She is breathing. She approaches people calmly and with patience. She has discovered there is no handbook on being the perfect anything in this world—parent, child, friend, teammate, female, teacher.

She has new goals: *Know myself. Be true to myself. Be genuine in every moment with every person. Perfection is not necessary.*

She feels she is well integrated into the world, competent. Her focus is on discovering the world within and the world without. She is not seeking groups. She is seeking herself. *To whom do I belong?* This is a question that no longer addles her mind. Dawning in her is a liberating thought: *Belonging is something you create with a world to which you were born belonging.*

SEEING BEAUTY

A word exists in the Sanskrit language whose meaning is critical to displaced children. The word is *sulochana.* Literally, sulochana means beautiful eyes. Figuratively it can mean *beautiful vision* or, *seeing the world as beautiful or good.* All things in life contain inherent beauty. But that latency is only brought to life by eyes capable of seeing beauty. Youth whose lives have contained great pain and ugliness may lose the capacity to see beauty. In that state, it does not matter how much beauty we place in their lives, not until we help them recover their ability to see it.

A child's mind must become used to the idea that she herself is beautiful. We cannot just say it to her over dinner one night and expect it to take hold. Her mind might be so accustomed to the idea that she is ugly, that it experiences the idea that she is beautiful as painful. Rain can take thousands of years to penetrate a rock. Negative identity can be just as unyielding a surface.

Physiological vision is not just a product of the eyes. The eyes receive imagery. The brain does the work of deciphering the light. This is another clue to the importance of mental transformation in youth. Through exposure and repetition, a change occurs in the way a child's brain processes the world. If she has lost the capacity to feel and decipher beauty, it is as though she encounters rose gardens and cannot tell them from patches of weeds. Our work is to bring color and vibrancy back into all aspects of her life. Then she can discern not only beauty, but also one unique form of beauty from the next.

Her ability to see beauty also derives from our ability to see beauty in her. Some children have *first-glance beauty*. Some have *second-glance beauty*. It depends on who is doing the looking. We see some children's beauty immediately. The aura smiles at us and we are taken in. Some children appear at first to be void of anything that would attract us. But when we look again we see something we first overlooked. This is second-glance beauty. Because all youth contain beauty it is up to us to learn to witness it during our first glance. With some of our young we need to go beyond looking at them. We need to look into them. This takes more effort. It yields more reward.

His heart journal: *Everybody looks at me. Nobody sees me.*

BODIES OF LIGHT

The Diné (Navajo) word *shonto* refers broadly to the light that reflects off water. Children need to see their reflections in the world. They also need to be *shonto*, the water-light that contributes to that reflection. Children have two kinds of bodies. One is a body of flesh and bone. The other is a body of light. The first body is much easier for them to see, so they tend to focus on it throughout their lives. It becomes the pole around which they spin and pivot. They use it to define themselves. It becomes an anchor that tethers them in a restrictive way.

If they attach too much of their beauty and worth to their physical body, they will spin in circles and remain unbalanced. Their body of light sets them free. This glowing formless beauty is their spirit, mind, and heart. As they begin to learn how to see this body, they slow their spin. They are becoming grounded. Their body of light does not cause them to spin, it causes them to expand. It gives them flight. It is the nature of sunlight. The more they are consumed within this body of theirs, the more they can go anywhere, do anything.

We help them visualize this body of light by regularly taking stock—along with them—of their intangible qualities. This simple practice of self-assessment creates the whole identity that opens youth up to their light. They have to learn to see this body. Some children come to it easier than others. This does not mean that some children have less light than others. Sometimes a great lamp is cloaked in a heavy shade. Shared exploration and surveying of internal beauty lift the shade.

THE CHILD IS A TEACHER

By virtue of their circumstances, children who have been uprooted from family were born to learn valuable lessons. This makes them natural teachers. Here is just a small part of the course syllabus on life they have to offer us:

◊ How to endure separation, uncertainty, and change

◊ How to trust adults with no previous ties to you

◊ How to believe after repeated betrayal

◊ How to attain self-worth even while standing out from family and peers

◊ How to detect anxiety, fear, and condescension in others

◊ How to manage the contradiction between love and prejudice in one's closest relationships

◊ How to carry the burden of stigma and stereotype

◊ The true meaning of family, beyond blood or legal bond

◊ How to forgive, overcome, heal, transcend

They have all these lessons to teach us. These youth are not dysfunctional so much as they are degreed. They have earned their wisdom hard and fast. We must help them release their lessons and become teachers. They were born to shine and our role is to help them see their light. Here is a message we can offer directly to them:

YOUR LIFE HAS A PURPOSE. Absolutely everything that has happened in your life has been shaping you to become the person you will be in the future. It may be hard to understand right now how every little thing will play a role in your life; but one day, when you look back at your past, it will all become clear. Even the difficult challenges will become things that you will use to become a better, stronger person.

The entire reason that you are experiencing a life that no one else is experiencing is because you are supposed to become a person that no one else can become. Your separation story has a purpose. Only you can discover what that is. Put your despair and longing in your heart-basket of purpose. It may save your life.

What makes you different truly does make you special, just as the things that make you like others also make you special. Your true beauty and value as a person come from this mix of being different in some ways and being the same in others. All you have to do is believe that one day your purpose will become clear and one day it will. You do not have to see your purpose now, you just have to believe and keep on walking strong. Even when times are hard know that . . .

YOUR PAIN HAS A PURPOSE. The pain that you have experienced in life may be difficult to deal with, but that does not mean that your pain is something negative. It is your *relationship* with your pain that can be positive or negative. You can allow your pain to darken your life or you can use it as a force to lighten your life and the lives of others. Learn how to transform your pain into power. This is the most valuable magic lesson you can learn.

Use your pain as a canvass for your creativity—paint a picture for the world of what your pain means to you and what other people's pain means to you. Pain is your opportunity to become more beautiful. Use your suffering to motivate your growth as a person, to become an adult who will not create that same pain in others. Even your pain has taught you lessons about life, which is why . . .

YOU ARE A TEACHER. Your experience as a child separated from family has made your life unique. This makes your life valuable and gives you a responsibility to share with the world what you have learned from your life. No one else is a greater authority on your life than you are. No adult knows more than you do about yourself. You are the expert. This is your chance to be a teacher.

Teach us what it means to be resilient and overcome the challenges you have faced. Teach us how you have been able to cope with the difficulties in your life. Teach us what it means to trust people when you have been betrayed by people. Teach us how you have managed to learn to love yourself even if you feel some people in your life have not loved you the way you needed.

Teach us how to heal from personal pain and become stronger. Teach us what it means to be compassionate and to care for others. Teach us why being sensitive to other people's feelings and their life background is important. Teach us how you have learned to believe in yourself and value yourself when other people sometimes have looked down on you. Teach us what the idea of family means to you. What it means to be there for each other. Teach us what makes children feel good about themselves and what makes them feel like they are truly part of a family.

You already have the highest educational degree possible in the subject of being you. We need your help to understand you, to better understand children, people, and life. We, the rest of the world, are your students. No matter what you end up becoming in life, each day you will have the opportunity, in the way that you live, to teach us!

His heart journal: *I too have been to the mountaintop. You would not believe the future I have seen. I have found the human heart. Follow me.*

COMPASSIONATE LEADERSHIP

As parents and advocates, our compassionate leadership involves learning to sing our own song to self and to the world. It involves learning to appreciate others singing their songs to self and to the world. We can lead youth in a way that does not feel as though we are bullying or belittling them. Even as we discipline them we can make them feel that we are uplifting them. Compassionate leadership leaves gentle footprints on children's hearts.

It is just as important that we teach our youth to become compassionate leaders. Such leadership plays a role in their healing and their growth.

Placing them in the role of being a mentor is a highlight of their compassionate leadership. When youth mentor other youth, a spring of pride and self-worth opens up in them. They may have never experienced someone looking up to them before, needing them. It is likely they have no idea that they have something to offer another. This can be a powerful healing experience and the beginning of a teacher- or leader-identity. A teacher and a leader live in every child. Circumstance and opportunity break open the shell to unleash this potential.

Healing internal wounds is the foundation of compassionate leadership. This healing dissipates blockage caused by fear and insecurity—the mortar of prejudice. Opening these blockages allows natural compassion to flow through. This flood facilitates the growth of a whole identity, a realization that we need others to thrive in order to reach our personal peak. This awareness provides the strength and courage necessary for children to lead themselves—the first and most elemental aspect of compassionate leadership. Courage is critical. Courage resists unhealthy conformity and drinks from the well of ancestral drumbeat. Truly courageous children follow their healthy instincts and say no to destructive impulses.

Compassionate leadership is a necessity because life requires constant re-imagining. Children need to be able to conceive of the life that may be beyond the life that is. They need to derive vision from the often obscuring mist of living and deliver that illumination to others.

Evidence glistens in young lives when compassionate leadership is at play. Such youth are internally self-rewarding and motivated. They have a clear sense of who they are, from where they are, and why they are. They honor, inspire, and see the beauty in others. Their creative gifts are flowing and they serve as muse to the creativity of their peers. They are humble teachers and proud, willing students. They are in love with life and fully able to live with love. Their song is unyielding and unapologetic. Others feel safe in their presence. Compassionate leaders make other children and people feel beautiful, even in the stormy eye of imperfection.

MISSING PONDS AND LEARNING

An important part of self-leadership is the ability to learn. Separation from family can jeopardize this ability. A subtle plague blows through a child's life in the form of missing family information. This information may contain vital insights into familial learning traits and patterns. Without this knowledge, it can be difficult to place youth behavior and school performance into a fair and useful context.

We may be unaware of biological family history regarding challenges with reading, information retention, information processing, attention, or other dynamics. Our tendency is to label these challenges as learning disabilities. It might be much more productive to call these *learning distinctions*. The way in which a child learns might be distinctive from most children, but it is not necessarily a function of lack of ability.

Without his family profile, it is easier to judge him as being deficient in intelligence, motivation, or ability. To counteract this missing family context he should receive competent and repeated learning assessment. Various challenges may emerge over time as his brain and chemistry evolve. Any identified challenges should be normalized. Tutoring and mentoring can be the bridge to discovering his optimal learning and teaching styles. Guidance from those who share his learning traits is an especially valuable esteem and role modeling source.

We may be unaware of biological family patterns of learning style that he might carry as strengths. He might, for instance, learn well through auditory means rather than visual; or through action versus discussion. He might be a social learner rather than a solitary learner. These strengths are also a part of his learning distinctions.

Without a biological family backdrop, our assumptions might more easily fail to recognize these latent strengths. His strengths should be identified early, both through formal assessment and through frequent creative self-expression opportunities. The arts, music, sports, and science are all vivid avenues for recognizing learning strengths. He needs to be asked what kinds of learning come easier to him or feel better to him. Encouraging his creativity is a wonderful form of asking.

His interests and inclinations are not to be dismissed. They tell us something of his learning nature. His biological family may be heavily inclined toward language and verbal stimulus, or toward numbers and quantitative processing. Or they might be artistic, mechanical, dramatic, or analytical. Without their presence, he has no context from which to validate his feelings and performance in areas inside and outside his inclination.

Providing him frequent opportunities for creative self-expression is like surrounding him with an orchard. When he picks mangos we do not label him as disabled for not picking apples. He might not meet our expectation with apples, but let him have his fill of mangos and he shows us he was a genius with fruit all along! Let's allow him to express his passions, and pay attention to how he chooses to spend his time. He might introduce us to his perfect day and perfect life.

Personality has an underrated role in the learning dynamic. Shy, quiet, loud, active: palettes upon which he mixes information for his paintings. The way he reads, writes, tests, analyzes, deduces—all intimately tied to his nature and demeanor.

Without his biological family as wallpaper, he has little or no opportunity to understand or validate his personality. Neither do we. We judge him according to our palette, our cultural standards. How can we decipher what is natural and what is problematic for him? He can create self-portraits in many ways. These self-portraits detail his personality traits and why he thinks he is the way he is. Writing, painting, drawing, acting, and music can all be used as exploratory methods, offering glimpses of his fundamental being.

TIME ORIENTATION OF LEARNING

Standard education involves a linear process: Do your homework, receive a grade. Take a test, receive a grade. Complete the year, graduate to the next grade. Complete enough grades, graduate from school. Feeling secure in this linear process requires a belief that good things will continue to happen if you do all the right things. It requires a confidence that each adult along the way will cause you good and not harm.

Many children do not fit this expected mentality. They experience a circular rather than linear existence. Each separation or trauma leaves them back at the beginning, faced with starting new relationships, healing another trauma wound, rebuilding esteem. The linear nature of the academic process conflicts with their circular lives. They lack faith in the idea that cumulative good deeds lead to good outcomes. They see school differently:

I Can't See the Prize. Trauma, separation, and chronic transition can leave children fixated on survival in the present moment. It can be difficult for them to conceive of the distant goal of graduating from high school or college. It pains them to endure the process of delayed gratification required by 12 or more years of schooling.

We can counter this by building opportunities for immediate gratification into their school experience.

Celebrate achievements regularly and widely within their social circle. Help them to recognize the links between their effort and the various rewards they ultimately receive from that effort.

I Can't Keep My Eye on the Prize. Youth may struggle to stay focused on educational expectations and tasks that do not yield immediately tangible results. Motivation, attention, and performance can be affected.

We can help them set short-term goals. Assist them in developing the habit of reflecting on their goals, dreams, passions, and life purpose. Creative self-expression, such as journaling, can be helpful. Celebrate achievements. Chart progress.

The Anxiety of Matriculation. A multitude of social and environmental changes are involved in the schooling process. Many of these transitions present challenges and post-traumatic triggers to children already sensitive to fragmented, temporary relationships. Some such changes include new teachers, new classmates, new friends, new assignments, changing schools within a grade, and changing schools between grades.

These transitions are eased when we focus on creative ways of helping a child maintain relationships across moves. Share examples of how change in relationships is normal for everyone in her life. Bonds that are temporary in terms of physical proximity offer us an opportunity to emphasize the emotional and spiritual permanence of bonds. We can tell her a story of forever love.

Displaced children were born to learn. They have life-dictated instincts, intuitions, curiosities, discernment, and judgment. They have survival skills: coping and resiliency abilities polished by their special journey through social relationships. They have tools that can be applied to their academics and social growth. Their drive toward confirming the truth and stability of their environment provides a motivation for learning. We can take advantage of this and translate their learning pulse into the healing acts of teaching, storytelling, being.

Here is a thought exercise: Describe three positive and three negative traits of your past, present, and future self. Write these traits down. Reflect on how you have grown, how you have failed to grow, and how you will need to grow in order to realize your future self. Create a list of growth factors and growth barriers. Finish by crafting a simple plan for how you will become your ideal self. This is an exercise we can teach youth as a stabilizing tool for their school and life transitions.

TRUE LITERACY

True literacy is the capacity *and* desire to know the world and the self *and* to use that knowledge. We can push *the basics* into a child all day at school, but if the material does not relate to his actual life he will not absorb it in a meaningful way. It will not light his internal fires. He needs to be shown how discovering his inner world can make his life easier. Seeing how knowledge of the outer world can relieve his inner pain and make his days brighter motivates him.

If we wish him to read and write we should feed him reading material and writing exercises that evoke his life. He hungers for cultural nutrition: substance that brightens his own reality, not that of someone to whom he does not relate. We should feed the artist. He cannot paint on empty. Reading and writing are tools for literacy.

Knowing there is a good payoff for self- and world-discovery are the fuel for literacy. Making these links visible, siphons the fuel into his curiosity tank.

The activities and exercises our youth engage in should be laced with cultural relevance. This means the moments should have something to do with their way of being, way of seeing. The more the experiences involve what youth care about, the more harmony they feel. Uprooted children may be sensitive to this harmony and disharmony. Culturally isolated children tend to think: *This activity isn't for me.* The moment becomes an empty exercise for someone else's benefit, not a personal moment with personal rewards.

When youth resist engaging in reading, writing, and creativity, we can offer an incentive. None of them is likely to enjoy emotional pain. Many of them are likely to be attracted to cars and money. It would be honest for us to tell them that literacy and creativity are medicine for their pain, keys to their car, and money in the bank. Creative self-expression is healing. It relieves pain. Even reading should be viewed as a creative experience. It involves personal interpretation and imagination.

Literacy creates mobility and opportunity, virtual vehicles to take youth where they want to go in life. Financial earning potential follows. When we point out how what moves them is connected to their creative and literary movement, we touch a motivating cord.

TEENAGE RISING

Inevitably, youthful growth and learning, or the lack of it, culminates in the precarious, precious season preceding adulthood. Here is where separation's impact often shows its fullest face, unearths its unpredictable holdings.

A sometimes startling transformation occurs during adolescence. Many of these changes are not inevitable. We cannot predict the degree to which they will occur. Often, the unique challenges of separation provide a child with the opportunity and motivation to self-reflect more than other children. Relatively placid personal development through the teen years can be a surprising consequence.

A youth's need to establish a unique identity apart from his existing family can create natural tension: between his need for uniqueness and his need for sameness. And tension between familial authority and his burgeoning self-authority.

His need to connect with his original family or cultural community roots often announces itself at this time. If his existing social circle has never been comfortable with those roots, it is likely to be much less so now that those roots are coming alive in him. Unaddressed fears and prejudice within his loved ones breed his new resentment. He loses faith that people truly love him. He feels they do not understand him. If they do not understand him how can they love him?

He withdraws from those he has lost faith in. A sense of shame descends upon him, separating him further from his relationships. At the thought of the social groups he now admires, he is shamed at the family and friends who are not members of that club. He does not want to bring those people dancing with him. He has found a whole new scene. He rejects his former scene, rejects his family and others who do not carry VIP status where he sees himself belonging now. His hurt is real. His spirit needs things and thrusts forward, crudely. His rejecting aura causes hurt in circles around him. Their hurt only deepens his sense of alienation: *There is too much friction and hurt here. I cannot belong to this.* This emotional cresting can leave him resenting his uprooted circumstance. As with many of us, he may direct his resentment toward those closest to him: family, friends, peers, and teachers. His need to feel normal in his family and community is a flint struck against his spirit's defiant lurch toward cultural dignity. Sparks fly as two strong flames fight each other within him. He wants to be embraced by everyone as normal and beautiful. He demands to be honored as distinctive and beautiful.

In the insecure chasm of his juvenile season he is tempted to see everything as rejection. His mind counts rose petals over and again: *She loves me, she loves me not. He loves me, he loves me not.* Social bonds grow exaggerated and fragile at the same time. In panicked moments, he tests his family's love for him. He tests everybody's love. This is what fear does. It is a frozen lake we walk, causing us to constantly stab at the ice with a stick to make sure we are not about to fall through. He keeps stabbing at people.

As his height increases, his shoulders broaden, and his voice deepens, he appears to others less like the cuddly boy they once found adorable. In their eyes, he has become formidable, intimidating.

He is becoming a sexual creature, gaining full access to human passions. Now this stigmatized youth triggers deep-seated prejudices and fear in others. He appears much more like a man and thus benefits less from our previously enamored affections. We view him now more as an equal in physical strength and overall ability. We are tempted by this equality to classify him quickly as either friend or foe. Sometimes his maturing form and function remind us of ourselves. This threatens us. We are projecting our own destructive power onto him and shuddering.

All of the usual adolescent drama can become overgrown in the greenhouse of separation circumstance. So much heat, humidity, and cloister. Our understanding of what gives rise to the drama is our best tool for riding out the storm. Maybe we should consult horsewomen and horsemen on this. They understand something about a strong creature that starts bucking. Those who have become skilled at creating harmony between rider and horse are likely to share similar stories. They have trained their bodies and minds to give leeway at certain bucking points, to assert force at other points.

Anger, frustration, and spite in return for a horse's bucking have never won a rider calm or respect from a horse. Harmony comes from understanding a rhythm, synchronizing to it. Not seeking to destroy the rhythm. Even as young people buck they are only trying to buck themselves into becoming the adults they know we already are. Their respect for us is waiting on a shelf behind the table where peace deals are made.

ADOLESCENCE AND BALANCING BEAUTY

A girl's apparent contradictions in balancing beauty are part of her healthy development process. Adolescence brings her into the flush of needing to establish a unique identity apart from her family. Her personal characteristics become magnified traits in a funhouse mirror. Much of what she sees in that mirror she wishes to deny. Some of what appears in the glass brings her a satisfaction only she can understand. She chooses to identify with that. *The rose she chose is the sweetest rose.*

Unpredictable currents run through her. She needs to connect with her original family roots. She needs to deny those roots. If we try too hard to encourage her in either direction, she resents us. Because we are so close to her, we are in the way of an intensely private becoming. Her becoming is a raw, exposed, vulnerable moment.

In her rawness she misguides her emotions. Resentment she has for her separation circumstances, she directs toward those now closest to her. Her feelings of rejection she turns into self-hatred. All her heart-colors run together. She screams for her own normalcy in her social world. She screams for acceptance and belonging. Even in the shrill of her voice is a rejection of that for which she longs: *These people, this place, it doesn't feel right. I can't see me here. I can't see me.*

Her costumes change, at times dramatically and often. Clothes, adornment, behavior . . . she is a novice, clumsily developing a personal repertoire for identifying with her chosen social groups. She and these groups play games with each other. They are awkward insecurity standing by the wall at the dance. So much shuffling, trying on each other: *This doesn't fit me. You'll look good in that.*

Membership doors are revolving madly. One day she is to be called Queen, the next she dresses in black. We can't keep up with her roster of friends. She screams to remind us of the latest peer who has been torn off the list. When beauty settles in a young soul, the trembles of change can be an earthquake. We may be the only thing standing steady, or not. We hold on tight when beauty tries on new clothes.

She may very well find her belongingness among others who don't belong. If we are threatened by this she knows it and the breach between us widens. We need to allow her certain identities as life-rafts over her waters. The identities may be seasonal. This does not invalidate them. Our own identity is seasonal: We rebirth it virtually every day and certainly with each significant experience.

She also needs us to allow her the time necessary to grow toward being able to make clear choices. She needs clarity in choosing which cultural aspects to adopt or not adopt from her new environment. She has decisions to make about which of her original cultural traits she will leave behind. Her cultural evolution is not passive. It involves conscious selections. The more we force these choices on her or deny her the space and time in which to make them, the more our relationship suffers.

Because she is beginning to resemble an adult she is becoming the target of hostilities reserved for adults. The broader family and community begin to unleash their prejudiced assault. When we embrace a child, what assaults her becomes our responsibility. We no longer get to say things like: *We don't pay attention to those things in our family. All people are the same.* Our wistful thinking days are over. The world's hostility is in our lap, a sick feline hissing at this child. Where is our response?

This changing beauty may withdraw from our family. She can see us as the force holding her back from taking flight. She does not quite know her destination yet but the ages have seeded her with a clock of self-determination. The clock alarm has begun to ring. She may feel shame over our family and reject our culture. We aren't what she came from. We are not who she gets to be herself around now. We are not where she is headed. So she tests our love. Although we are not any of these things, we are something priceless to her. We are forever a place she will turn to when her wings grow tired and she has to land.

Through all of this she is simply enacting the usual adolescent drama. Her separation shadow, though, has tripped the lights and intensified the play.

Here is a thought exercise for increasing our compassion to the balancing of beauty and the youthful changing of *clothes*: Create a list, in descending order, of the seven most important aspects of your life. Ask an exercise partner to do the same. Discuss with your partner the differences and similarities in your two lists. Discuss how these aspects make up your cultural (whole) identity—the person you see yourself as being. Share with each other how you would be affected as each of those seven aspects were damaged or removed from your life. Now remember the child. Life has demanded repeatedly that she give up her seven beauty clothes. People have demanded. Are we one of those people? Can we understand the anxiety and loss she feels at the changing of her clothes?

MYTHS OF ADOLESCENCE AND FAMILY

Not every adolescent wishes to become legally wed to a permanent family. Maybe it would help us if we think about what our closest friends mean to us. In many ways they are a permanent family to us. But do we wish to be legally bound to them in such a way that we cannot have other close friends in our life? We have a social bias for crowning people as parents to a child and simultaneously decreeing that other people can no longer be parents to that same child.

Yes, children want permanent families. But what does this mean? Our truest friends remain permanently a part of us. Our own legally decreed families sometimes fade in and out of our lives. At some point, a child determines that what he really wants is family that feels good to him. He does not want that joining to impair his opportunity to have even more family that feels good to him. He cannot have too much healthy, safe, caring family.

Legalized entry into a family does not represent permanency to him. He has had adults break covenants with him all his life. Relationships full of honesty, consistency, and mutuality represent permanency to him. He will see his foster, kinship, friendship, and mentoring relationships as permanent if they contain the elements that make him feel beautiful and as though he belongs.

He will see his legalized family as temporary if it feels unsafe, as though its nature does not allow him to sink his roots into it. Our obsession with legally creating family and non-family distinctions in his life should be replaced with a devotion to creating healthy, honoring relationships in his life. Legal permanency is not always superior to the permanency of health within other forms of relationship.

If he does not come into a legally permanent family before the end of his childhood, this does not mean that he will not develop a permanent family in his adulthood. Even if he never has children or is married, he has the opportunity to develop permanent kinship. This is dependent upon how we have helped him develop the capacity to engage in healthy relationships.

He wishes and needs the blessing of family, in whatever form, to remain with him into his adulthood and throughout it. At what age do we expect these youth to become independent of a support circle? Look at us. We never stop leaning on ours. We pass through our elder years still holding on dearly to family. This boy becoming a man would like a family of some form around him through and beyond his transition. He does not turn 18 and suddenly wish to be alone in the world.

We also tend to believe that older children are more difficult to incorporate into families than younger children. In many cases the opposite is true. They may have clearer understanding of the kind of family that is best for them. Older children also have a greater ability to articulate their thoughts and feelings. This can increase our understanding of their needs and nature. They often have more developed coping skills for such a transition.

And in that their friendship circle is usually broader and more central to their life, they are not as dependent on family for a sense of self. This leaves them more able to offer reciprocity in the flow of family life.

The idea that adolescents are too damaged by that age to be good candidates for a new family is a notion born of fear. The truth is that many of them have already engaged in healing processes, largely through their friendships and creative self-expression. This may grant them a stability they did not have at a younger age.

We often take any conflict older children have in their new families as evidence of a bad placement. What frequently follows is the removal of the child from the family. The conflict though might be a function of natural adolescent transformations. If we were to look deeply and without judgment we might find that the conflict may be even greater in another family. At times youth need their imperfect family more than ever.

Adolescents are not blinded by self-absorption, as we may imagine. This season of their lives is saturated with extreme concern for the well-being of their friends, the world, and, yes, even their family. Their compassion commonly erupts into panic, anxiety, and anger. If we understand compassion as the root of their eruption, we better equip ourselves emotionally and otherwise to be there for them in the way they need us to be.

It is easy for us to assume that adolescents are too old to reap the benefits of a new family. The child we once were lives in our heart and mind forever. Throughout our lives we are affected by our family in much the same way we were as children. Uprooted children are no different. Family benefits do not gauge our age.

We fluctuate between believing that adolescents know enough to be on their own and feeling that they are too young to know what is best for them. Our uncertainty matches the cloudiness of their transformation. This is a breeding ground for conflict. The very idea that they are either ready or unready for the world is a myth. They are both. They flirt with certainty and regress into fear. They shed old habits and then fall back into them as if into the comforting arms of an old lover.

Our challenge is to behold them as fluid: moment to moment, day to day, and season to season. In order to achieve harmony with them we have to be fluid. Their adolescence forces us to grow. This is obvious. Not as obvious is the beauty of this manner of growth. It is a growth that tests and fills the gaps in our wholeness.

GANGS

Affiliation into groups is a natural human inclination. Gang involvement is a gurgle of water from a pool of natural instinct. That youth would be attracted to the lures that gangs offer should not surprise us, especially to the degree that youth lack those aspects in their lives. The lures include familial acceptance, validation, friendship, belonging, protection, and social stature.

We adults commonly join gangs of a sort. We call them by other names: political parties and lobbies, faiths, clubs, teams, organizations, and so on. Our adult groups can exact even greater social damage than do the gangs of our youth. Understanding is gained by reflecting on what drives us toward unhealthy attachments to certain groups.

The elements we identify will largely be the same elements driving our youth toward gangs.

From this understanding we can derive strategies for filling the lives of youth with the substance they search for in gangs. We can fill our own lives with the same. Together we can be free of unhealthy group attachments.

Negative peer pressure preys on desperate minds. Fragmented identities leave youth feeling as though they have limited options for belonging. Such identities create fences on the horizon where none exists. Like a frightened colt, a youth will not even approach the horizon to see how far the land stretches. He stays in place and shivers in the cold of his self-limitation. He is a free colt caged.

If a youth does not see that he has other places to go, other friendships to fall into, he will perceive that the cage door before him is closed. He will feel trapped and believe he has no choice other than to participate in what his harmful peer pressure drives him toward. We open the door of his perception by convincing him the whole world is his to play with. Where people belong he belongs. The cage door is open.

Young people create their circles of belonging in as many ways as their imaginations allow. Desperation increases the flock of unhealthy fantasies. For a pubescent girl, a doorway of possibilities has opened. She may feel that having babies is a way for her to create a family she believes will not leave her. This is her mother-baby gang. Her instincts are good. Her impulse is unfortunate. We can work on both with her.

We can help her to understand the nature of relationships—how some are meant to endure and some have their season. We can help her to identify the people in her life who truly care. We can assist her in seeing that having a baby under her circumstances might actually increase the chances of a separation between her and the baby—just the opposite of what she is hoping for. This is a conversation that can unfold in a safe space void of criticism, judgment, and blame.

Gangs, like all groups, evolve according to the aura of each particular member. Youth can individually influence the groups in which they participate. They have to be taught that they hold this constructive and destructive power. Avoiding membership in negative groups does not have to be the only goal. Changing groups from within is possible. Many gangs have been moved away from violence and self-destruction and toward social productivity. Visionary leadership, even by young people, can make this true.

SELF-MUTILATION

A young lady cuts and burns herself. We cannot believe this horror. Our only panicked thought is that she must need therapy. She may. She also may simply need to have her pain acknowledged, validated, understood. Desperate acts tell of a desperate situation. But where is the story unfolding? Inside of her? Around her? At school? She needs us to become detectives and discover where her true desperation is erupting.

We might reflect on the many ways we hurt ourselves. We smoke, drink, drug, overeat, drive unsafely, spew anger at each other. We fill our hearts with hatred and soak our internal body with fear. We damage our organs with stress and block our love from flowing with boulders of prejudice. Are these ways any less destructive than a child's? Are we not mutilating ourselves? We have learned to enact our mutilation in more subtle ways. The damage is still there. Where is our therapy?

A child's mutilation can appear more gruesome. Maybe this is because she has fewer options. Having less control over her life in her world of adults, her desperation forces itself out through narrower openings. The result is a more forceful expression. We can look at this in another way. Her mutilation may be a sign that she is *being* mutilated. She is being mutilated by her experience in our family and community; and by the failure of her circle to see her. Her voice is blocked and she is dying to let out a cry, a song, anything that calls us to attention.

When we find ourselves in an abusive relationship what quickly follows is that we begin to abuse ourselves. The ways may be inconspicuous. This is the strangeness of harm. We create self-defeating habits when exposed to hurtfulness. We begin to mirror or replicate the harm being done to us. We pick up the hammer the abuser left and start beating ourselves. We place our own head on the anvil of suffering.

When we see a girl mutilating herself our first horrified thought is: *What is wrong with her?* Our best first thought might rather be: *What is wrong in her world? She is being mutilated.* Now we are walking down a more productive road. What do you do when you are drowning in the ocean? You hysterically scream for help. You frantically flap your arms. Why? You are trying to get anybody, anything in the world to notice you are dying. Children do this too in the clutches of their own dying.

What does a destructive state represent? It is a desperate striving for power, control, predictability, dominance. Why? To counter the pain and chill of perceived aloneness and powerlessness. If we are aware of these roots of self-destructive behavior we can move beyond simply punishing our children for their acts and attitudes. We can work with them to change the conditions that create their aloneness and powerlessness.

Some youth will bury their heritage far deeper than even fearful others wish they would. That is how badly they are dying to fit in. Literally dying. To be so repulsed with one's inheritance, to so urgently denounce that endowment, takes a perverse kind of dying. This too is self-mutilation.

Allowing a child to grow up despising her own heritage is true neglect. Actively seeding her with a devalued idea of her origins is the truest of abuses. Self-rejection is a tortured existence, to which material poverty cannot compare. What does it matter if a youth is fed three times a day if her spirit is starved of its own dignity? Self-love, which implies a love of the origins of self, is a sustenance we cannot deny.

SUBSTANCE ABUSE

We are all in love with intoxication. We turn to romance, thrills, danger, poetry, and music. Our entire world is a calabash of addicts scurrying for their fix. That our young are tempted by intoxication is not the problem. The trouble is that our marketing campaign is weak, while sellers of death and poison run a strong promotion.

Each drug that comes into fashion is simply a new name for an old game, the game of escape, disengagement, false control, and putting pause to the pain. Punishing drug use without changing the life conditions at the source of this destructive impulse can be counterproductive.

In essence, all of life is a drug. Acquainting youth to the truly beautiful drugs is our challenge. Once they understand how good it makes them feel to dance, sing, write, and create, they become addicted. As they become familiar with the highs of achievement, leadership, mentoring, and compassion, they become fixated. Our labels and languages for what is a drug and what is not take us away from the resolution. We can redefine the term *intoxicant* to include every single thing right or wrong—from the rose to the sky to the song. Now we can go about discerning unhealthy from healthy intoxication.

SLOW SURRENDER

A slow surrender to pain and despair can carry a child away from us and away from life. We have to look deeper to see this kind of passive suicide. It is not an intentional dying. It is surrender. We surrender to age. A child surrenders to pain. To be aware of this kind of dying requires a gathering of our will. It is very difficult to confront people about their dying. No one wishes to see it. Not us. Not the child. Although we may give this process other names, the destination is the same. Eventually the physical body will join the spirit that has long since faded.

If we can summon the courage to take action, we may be able to change the life conditions that are causing this tragedy. Relationships are vital. Each is an irrigation trench allowing healing waters to reach the parched heart. Relationships allow access to healing. If relationships within the family are not sufficient, together we can go searching for the relationships that will infuse youth with the will and nutrients for healing.

Slow surrender can mask itself as many things: destructiveness, withdrawal, anger, mimicry. The more a child mimics others and seems to have no real self, the greater her surrender. There is too much pain in the place her self inhabits. She stops going there. Until she finds the tools to make going there less horrifying, less helpless, she will stay away. The tools are delivered through reflection ponds, in the form of relationships, wrapped in packages of trust and safety.

A child slowly, painfully finds his voice, recovers his echo from the canyons of his life. There are moments when he is very willing to slip away from this living, because his song is a whispered thing, as though it is calling to him from a place other than this one. The line between his outcome and those of his peers is thinner, more fragile than we may imagine. The blessing is that the spirits of our young are often so strong, stronger than our own adult imperfections that bring them so many wounds. We can bury their song in the desert of our alienating world, bury that song even for years, and still it can remain alive, waiting. The proper wind picks it up and carries it, whistling, into its debut.

ANGER

Yelling, screaming, and cursing are not anger. They are behavior. Anger is the burning inside our heart. It is the flames that creep out from the vat of our woundedness and singe our sensitive inner clothing. Anger is a scab we scrounge up to protect the wound. It is ugly and malformed but often it is the best we can do on the spot and under the circumstances.

The less our healing resources, the more we abide anger to keep away even the slightest breeze that would awaken our hurting. We learn this habit in childhood when our wounds too often go unprotected by adults and unarticulated by our limited tongues. It becomes the one thing we may wield on our bleeding behalf that seems to give us reprieve from suffering.

Little do we know that we are making friends with a habit that will burn us from the inside out, its acid an irony of destruction more willful than the wounds that leave us willing to farm anger as our misguided crop. We cannot teach children to unlearn their anger without first giving them other tools with which to defend and express themselves. Nor can we expect them to shed this habit if we continue to wear anger as our own skin. We cannot model anger and expect them to leave anger behind. This shedding should be a team resolution.

Anger is a habit a child learns from adults. She learns that it is a way to both express and protect self. It grows in her the more she feels unable to control her life. She discovers that taking care of animals makes her feel safe and is a way to express her nature. Falling further into this sweet space she experiences release. She becomes less dependent upon anger. Caring for animals becomes her shield, a way of protecting her heart, and finding shelter from hurtful people. The tenderness she and the animals share with each other grows into a vibrant song. She has found her expression. Children will only abandon anger when they discover new shields and tools.

One of the most difficult things for a young person to do is locate the origin of his anger. His pain overflows inside, builds into pressure that vents itself almost randomly. He displaces his rage. Everyone and every circumstance becomes a target he blames for his suffering. We can help him by having him work backward to trace his chain of events and feelings. He can do this in writing if not verbally. His challenge is to identify what caused him to feel which way, to develop an injury timeline.

He has to understand that unless he discovers the source of his anger, his anger will never leave him. Once he realizes this, he may be motivated to end his suffering.

Identifying the origins is much like genealogical work—a tree with branches waits for him to track it down. As those branches take shape in his mind he gains awareness of the steps he needs to take to resolve his anger. Each time he is able to locate a particular origin, usually rooted in hurt, he strengthens his skill and habit for locating his anger. He is on the way to self-control and self-healing.

MANTRAS

Compassion frees us from the shackles of anger and vengeance. Freedom is the offspring of compassion. Here are some simple mantras that, practiced consistently, can create the habit of compassion in young people. These repeated meditative thoughts can also help develop healthy attitudes and self-healing capacity:

Who makes me suffer suffers.

Who attacks me has been attacked.

Who is withdrawn once called out and was beat down.

My anger hurts me more than anyone.

My deep breath is my escape.

My understanding sets me free.

I am loved.

I am Love.

Many of these sayings can be just as useful to us. We can create our own mantras at any time to fit the situation. Their effectiveness relies on the basic law of repetition as a force for mental and emotional change. World-class athletes and performers use mantras to great effect. The sayings may even seem simplistic to us, to the point of embarrassment. Fortunately we can recite them silently!

Here is a useful mantra to teach youth: *I have to shine what's mine.* This is a message about considering one's own blessings to be sufficient. It also speaks of a responsibility to polish what one has into what one desires. We all possess light; we just have to learn to let it shine. And *the light that is mine* is sufficient for every youth. Imagine them believing: *I do not need to resent or be jealous of others for their own blessings. I only have to shine what's mine.*

A PORCUPINE IN HAND

A wild animal bares her teeth at us for three reasons: she feels cornered, she feels we are a threat, or she feels she has something (her offspring) to protect. A child bares her teeth at us for the same reasons. A kind soul in an insensitive home or classroom becomes a porcupine in time. Her quills are all she has to back us off from attacking her nature.

How do we get her to see that she is not cornered, that she is safe and has exit options? What do we do to become friend and not enemy in her eyes? How can we help her feel that her own vulnerable possession, her heart, is not in danger? Our answers to these questions are what put her snarling teeth away. Each of us can derive our own answers. What matters is that we ask the right questions.

For instance, we assume friendship and family would be appealing possibilities to her. But from the clenches of her woundedness, family and friendship might be seen as means for others to get close enough to hurt her again. *She sees enemies.* We can work with her on the difference between healthy and unhealthy relationships. Her suspicion and fear are entry points for our conversation.

This message pertains equally to us as to our youth: To say to yourself, *I wish to grow*, but then cut yourself off from those who may be able to teach you is self-defeating. Unnatural individualism is a burial exercise. Believing that you can get away with harming the world and others is self-deception. The world is an inescapable whole, not a mass of pieces. When you cut life and reality into pieces, everything that you cut bleeds. You bleed most of all because all the pieces exist *within* you. No one has ever found peace by fragmenting life.

DEFIANCE

She who sees wolves everywhere will exist as if she is always about to be attacked. An entrenched identity has taken hold as a result of persistent feelings that she is an outsider. All around are people she feels do not understand her experience or how it has shaped her. In order to endure the cascade of pain this brings, she develops a resistant attitude that says: *I don't need anybody. I'm tired of being put down, rejected, criticized. I'm going to do whatever I want, act however I wish.* This defiance is angry and defensive. It should not be confused with being true to oneself.

She becomes so dependent upon her defiance that she will not let anyone in. The more we tell her we mean no harm the greater her defensive rage.

She may identify herself with others who share her separation story or distinctive heritage. But even this affiliation can grow extreme and destructive. She is forming an angry club with high castle walls. The insularity smothers everyone inside the walls. Hot tar is poured on everyone standing outside.

With a sharp tongue and indolent behavior she constantly tests us. She wants to see whether or not we truly respect her, how far our patience will extend. Not knowing the boundaries of our loyalty causes great anxiety. In some ways she feels better finding reason to designate us *enemy* than she does wondering about our motivations. Once she has named us *enemy* she has clarity. Her defiance is partly a plea for us to prove our love by fighting through her resistance. As she flails she is saying: *Show me how much you care. Show me your courage. How much of my bruising are you willing to take?* Perhaps most of all she wants our understanding. Even she does not understand her turmoil. Past letdowns have rendered her virtually incapable of believing we can understand.

Our challenge is to read between the lines of her bared teeth. In her attitude and behavior are certain questions. She is pleading: *What is in your heart?* She seeks our substance, beyond that of our authority. *What are you all about?* Her defiant heart is a frightened heart. Uncertainty cripples her. She is on a crude quest to discover our core values, motivations, life history. She does not do well going through the motions with strangers.

Why are you here? Until we show her clearly why we care about her in particular and about an uprooted child in general, she cannot rest. What is driving us toward her? If we have not reflected on this we will have a hard time providing the reasons she needs.

One of the trusted rocks she catapults over her wall at us is the statement: *You don't know me.* With these words she rejects the power she perceives in us, and in others, that has been imposed on her life. She rejects the long rain of prejudice and assumption that people have drenched her with ceaselessly. With *You don't know me,* she rationalizes her behavior, gives herself secret excuses she will not reveal. This concealment is a small power for her. She holds it tightly.

You don't know me. These words allow her to manage her trust and distrust. She doesn't even know if she believes what she is saying but she tries out the words anyway. It gives her time to decide how much to let us in. Most of all, *You don't know me* is a shield with which she masks her wounds. Her heart is truly saying: *I am hurting and you have no idea how badly.*

Defiance may confound us. Ways exist to cool this flame. Our responses to *You don't know me* are one of those ways. We can offer her: *No, I don't know you. But I owe you my best effort to understand you.* Or, *You don't know me either. But here we are together. What are we going to do?* It is vital that we acknowledge her authority over her own experience. Too many people have prejudged and presumed with her.

Whatever we wish to convey to her, we should try to wrap in a more appealing package, such as with a smile or with humility. A child who wants nothing more than genuine respect is more likely to receive our offering. Confrontational approaches to her result in confrontation. Problem-solving (creative de-escalation) approaches leave open the possibility of productive outcomes.

When she raises her voice or shows anger or agitation this is a reaction to her pain, fear, and even her intimidation by the situation or by us. Her chest-puffing behavior is a defensive response to vulnerability, not evidence of strength or confidence. If we understand this, our reaction to her bristling will be less defensive. Our defensive responses only sharpen her defiance, driving us both further into conflict.

It is important that we breathe in these moments. Thinking honestly of ourselves at her age can provide calming perspective. Focusing on her strengths, gifts, and unique beauty can be challenging when she is attacking or resisting. But it can provide us immeasurable relief. The minute we start seeing her as a monster because of her monstrous behavior, we begin treating her as a monster. Beauty has never grown from attacking the beast.

When we are anxious or overwhelmed, it may be best to let her be the teacher. She can reveal new perspectives and ideas to us. We have to show her that we care to learn from her. The invitation is simple: *Teach me. I don't consider myself to be an expert on your life or culture, but I am willing to learn about those things. Teach me.*

Certain questions can be helpful: *What is the real issue here?* We should ask this of her and of ourselves. *How do you suggest we resolve this?* This partially turns over power and control to her. *What do you want out of this?* This helps her to focus on being constructive and expressing her grievance rather than her anger.

Together with her we should focus not on the rules and policies that might be aggravating her, but on the purpose and objective of those conditions. With every idea, action, or resolution we identify we should be asking: *How will this help her? How will it help us?* She is naturally self-interested. We can take advantage of this by identifying outcomes to which she will relate. Can we get her to ask: *How does my family's well-being benefit me?* We can help her answer, in ways that feel good to her, the question: *Why should I care about my growth as a person?* And, *How can I go about making this positive growth happen? What's my plan?*

Right behavior and *wrong* behavior are standards that mean little to some. Youth with low self-worth do not respond well to appeals to morals and responsibilities. Despair, anger, and hopelessness do not leave much room to consider right and wrong. When we touch young hearts (what they care about) they are more likely to respond.

Appeals to the broken, small self may have little success. When we appeal to the whole, big self, youth gain a sense of worth even as we ask them to stretch past their comfort zone. We are suggesting to them their purpose and value as we request their growth. On the surface they may scorn our compliments. Inside they cannot help but feel good hearing they are valuable to the team, whatever team that is. This is how we appeal to the heart.

When a young person approaches us with contrary attitudes, we should not take the bait. There is no need to continue cycling the argument. When he is aggressive, we respond with calm strength and physical distance. If he tries passive behavior, we are assertive but share power. When he yells, we redirect his energy creatively, toward physical activity, perhaps. Yelling back at him is an obvious fuel to his fire.

If interaction between us is chronically conflicted, we can take time away from each other. We can explore other people as a complementary presence in his life. Sometimes his experiences with others will increase his appreciation of us. When he disrespects us, we need not disrespect him in return. Instead, we can teach him how disrespecting others in fact hurts him in return.

We might interpret his anger as the flag of emotional pain and proceed from that understanding. We should trust our instincts. Compassion reveals the right thing to do. We may interpret his resistance as a sign of fear or an exertion of power. In response, we seek to reduce his fear or to create in him a sense of healthy power.

The language we use with him can unlock defiant doors. Creating a new language can pay great dividends. Instead of starting our sentences to him with: *You have* to—, we can try: *We need you to*—. Instead of: *You should*—, *You might want to*— might be less agitating. His defiant nerves are raw. Our skilled language and careful consideration are not passivity and deference on our part. We are simply avoiding lighting matches around a flammable heart.

Youth who hold little material or social power in their lives will seek to acquire and exercise power when they perceive an opportunity. Or they will shy away from the chance to assert power. They may even react in both ways at varying times. Our reflection on this unpredictable dynamic may yield helpful ideas. We can learn how to take advantage of youths' relationship with power.

One promising step is to explain to a defiant child that the power differential between us is a necessary function of our responsibility as an adult: We are charged with guiding him and using our experiential insight. But we have no desire to control him, nor do we feel he is less capable or intelligent than us. In fact, the more he grows the more power he will acquire over his own life.

We should always apologize to him for any inappropriate tone, words, or response that we use with him. He may have driven us to it, but these are moments in which it is important for us to model taking responsibility for our imperfections. Unless we achieve humility and acknowledge our mistakes directly to him, we are hypocritical in expecting him to do the same.

He needs our support and encouragement as he practices admitting his mistakes to himself and others. He may be unfamiliar with admitting mistakes without that confession immediately being followed by reprimand or punishment. He needs a positive association between apology and outcome.

All this volatility and tension can unleash our own unrelated issues. They shoot up through the fissures of the moment and rain molten heat on a young and astounded soul. He has no idea what he has triggered in us. We may not even understand. But we are boiling. Now we need to stop and ask inwardly: *Is my reaction about him or about my own woundedness?* It helps if we try to identify what exactly about him triggers exactly what response in us. If we can locate our root sensitivity, when it is threatened we have a chance to soothe it.

Often we assume he means certain things by his actions and words. We draw upon our own intent when we act in similar ways. Then we project that intent onto him. We may be well off the mark. Our reaction, based on that mistaken assumption, takes us both into greater conflict. When, in a cooler moment, we ask him what he was thinking and feeling at the time of his defiance, we open a two-way door for understanding.

Just as he may internalize the attitudes of others, we may internalize his. We become more aware when we ask: *Why am I reacting this way? Have I taken on his emotions or attitudes?* We can create a journal record of his behavior and how it precipitates our emotions and thoughts. This allows us to see patterns in the relationship. We can list our actual responses and our ideal responses. We can list how we would prefer him to act and then share this with him. Doing this work, our vulnerabilities and areas for growth are revealed. As we acquire this self-awareness skill we can teach it to him. Defiance and conflict are windows behind which true needs wave out to us.

PUNISHMENT AND DISCIPLINE

Pity does not produce dignity. Youth need our empathy (understanding) not our sympathy. Understanding is not the same thing as giving them an excuse for their behavior. Understanding is a flash of connection that allows effective prevention and intervention. Excuses don't produce responsibility. Pointing out youths' destructive and constructive power in the world may help them accept a sense of responsibility.

Appealing to youths' whole identity, the sum of what's inside them, motivates personal change. Discipline should be designed to activate their whole identity. If they do not see the connection between being disciplined and their potential, they may imagine discipline as nothing other than more unfairness and cruelty.

Many displaced youth assume their relationships will end as soon as they misstep. They can experience discipline as a prelude to their relationship being terminated with school, classmates, family. Discipline should be administered and explained as affirmation of their potential and the high expectations held for them. We should clearly represent rules of conduct as functions of personal growth and not as red flags for personal flaws.

Allowing youth to help create the rules of conduct and discipline is empowering. When they feel they have had a voice in the process, they are more likely to respect discipline that is later enacted. Their behavior and attitudes may improve because they do not wish to violate the standards they played a role in creating.

It is important that we explain the purpose of each particular behavioral guideline and related discipline. The purpose should clearly relate to and benefit youth and not only their family, classroom, or community.

Once youth grasp their own interest in conduct and discipline they can grant those guidelines at least grudging respect. They may even surprise us and become advocates of these rules to their peers. This is ownership.

JUVENILE JUSTICE AND DISCIPLINE

Bullying youth with our ego and anger is not how to be hard on crime. This is like saying stomping weeds is being hard on weed growing. Weeds do not care if we stomp them, as long as we do not destroy their roots. Weeds know that as long as they have their roots they can keep rising, keep throwing wild parties.

Crime does not care about our vengeful need to punish youth. Crime knows that as long as we do not destroy its roots it will rise up again. The roots of crime are alienation, despair, clouded identity, and a longing to assertively express pain. We have a choice: Do we go on punishing our youth and congratulating ourselves for believing we are being hard on crime? Or do we, by administering hard discipline that involves healing, education, healthy relationships, and growth, kill off the roots of crime within our youth?

Sometimes to be hard on the weeds growing from our youth we have to be compassionate to the suffering and self-blindness that plague their existence.

Fundamental questions have to be asked perpetually: Are we invested in rehabilitation or punishment and institutional segregation? We seem to never have committed to a path. Our wavering diminishes our effectiveness. Is our objective to protect the community from the child or the child from the community? A holistic wisdom would argue both are true. The child *is* the community. The community *is* the child.

When a child is exposed to the juvenile justice system a thread in the fabric of family and community is pulled. Given enough exposures, this fabric unravels. This makes recidivism a high priority. Our best juvenile justice is a process that fosters growth and healing in both our youth and our community. Are growth and healing not the best form of protection?

When we punish our youths' behavior the punishment itself can bear many harmful offspring. Beating down youth who have already been damaged by previous beatings tends to create more pain, anger, trauma, and death of spirit. Self-beating minds receive punishment not as a motive to improve but as further evidence of their worthlessness. Children who feel this way about themselves do not respond to punishment in the way we might. They do not grow stronger or act better. They become more broken, more soaked in despair.

There is no reason we cannot highlight their strengths even as we address their misgivings and challenges. If our true objective is to build them up, we should avoid tearing them down as a function of correcting their behavior. Nurturing is not coddling, it is strengthening.

When we institutionalize youth in order to punish we create generational loss in our families and communities. We segregate entire populations of young behind walls and wire and away from the relationships our communities need to naturally replenish themselves.

We are creating future parent absenteeism. Our kept youth are practicing being absent. Absent from their families. When they become parents the one skill they will have spent the most time polishing is the skill of being absent.

This includes the mothers who were once punished girls. A mother can be absent even when she is physically present. Have you ever been in a relationship in which the other person just was not there? For a while you pretend the physical body is companion enough. Then you realize you are role playing with a puppet. Beneath its form there is no person. Your aloneness becomes glaring. Eventually you realize this is no relationship. This is the inheritance we prepare for our future generations by punishing our current generations rather than disciplining them.

When we isolate to punish, our youth are forced to practice existing in isolation. This does not lead to skills or mentalities for existing in society. These skills and mentalities have to be practiced. We are polishing our young into social insufficiency.

When we practice institutional anger as a society, this only improves our skill of administering institutional anger. It brings us no closer to understanding our youth and their struggle. It does nothing to facilitate their healing or ours. Administering and receiving punishment shuts down the cerebral frontal cortex, in which our creativity and reasoning take place. This is the problem-solving region that youth require to repair themselves and that we need to become better shepherds.

Giving and receiving punishment activates the primitive part of our brain, the generator of panicked survival surges. This part of our brain does nothing but incite us to anger and belligerence. This is the brain that has built our culture of punishment. We congratulate ourselves for this inflamed cycle. It leads us nowhere but toward larger populations of angry penned up youth and a society increasingly angry at our angry youth.

Our concentric human circles are shattered against the hard rocks of punishing societies. Child and family are separated. Family and community are separated, for the family whose children are punished becomes the family scorned. When enough families within a community suffer this fate, that community becomes separated from society. See how we look down on that which loses its treasures? A family becomes *that* family. A community becomes *those* people: the ones whose children are bad, whose parents are bad, the ones who deserve bad things. Maintaining a system of punishment requires continual justification. We have to label the offenders— the children, families, and communities—until they become non-human and worthy of our angry lash. Do we realize that the world of humans looks down upon societies that do little more than lock up their youth in multitudes? This is the last ring broken in the circle: the punishing society becomes separated from humanity.

Some of us are convinced more by money than by morals. Even our money is touched by a culture of punishment. Our system becomes overburdened. We cannot build enough facilities, hire enough staff, pay enough in salaries, budget enough utilities. Our workers become stressed, angry, threatened, and unhealthy. Morale declines. Ineffective workers and teams lose hope and spirit. So do ineffective leaders.

We call our criminal containment systems *Departments of Correction*. They are not called *Departments of Punishment* for a reason. At some point these systems were imagined as structures for correcting behavior. Certainly our systems for juveniles were conceived as correctional. Vindictive treatment in response to youthful transgression was not the ultimate objective. The worse and more frequent the criminal acts of our youth, the more vindictive we have become. Especially to youth who swim outside of our most influential mainstreams. Our adult maturity is being tested. Do we possess the fortitude to remain corrective?

When the flow of youth into the chambers of punishment becomes a flood, all the building we do to house the offenders is not enough. At some point we have to stop the flow, try a new paradigm. Do we have the will to stop pushing out our chests and instead try expanding our hearts? Sharpening our vision? If not, we risk a great flood with no high ground for our escape.

THE IMPORTANCE OF RITUALS

Discipline, healing, and growth are parts of the circle of positive youth development. This circle is solidified by concrete experiences that anchor youth within their change process. The importance of rituals, traditions, and rites of passage should not be overlooked. These critical habits help youth connect their heritage with aspects of their daily life. They are reminders of self, purpose, and origin—a shade tree against the glare of confused identity.

Structure and direction are additional benefits of rituals. In our chaotic, high stimulus world, children are prone to becoming overwhelmed and lost. In such states they are more vulnerable to negative peer pressure. They lose sight of their own beauty and seek to appropriate the beauty of others. Rituals and traditions are that song urging: *Dear child, remember who you are.*

Rites of passage and daily rituals are critical requirements for creating whole identity, reflection ponds, and beauty and belonging. These actions, which can be adopted by classrooms and youth groups as well as families, create mental habits, bonding, and celebration of worth. We can derive the content of our rituals from cultural traditions as well as from contemporary realities. Rituals cement desirable values and filter out the effects of harmful social messages. Rituals provide habitual cleansing and irrigation, lessening the need for corrective discipline and clinical therapeutic attention.

STORYTELLING AND ELDERS

One of the most enduring, humanistic rituals of all is storytelling. Storytelling is a tremendous door of opportunity standing before us, one we often neglect to enter. We can share with youth how we were raised, how we stumbled and fell, and how we overcame. We are providing a blueprint, a topographical map exposing the ups and downs of our terrain. Our stories connect the points of our life and reveal how we developed our values.

Our young need to see the process of our becoming, and not just the endpoint. Too many times we adults show only our finished face. We leave so many priceless lessons in the drawer of our teaching desk.

Storytelling normalizes change and struggle. We are so good as humans at cloaking our challenges that we can appear robotically composed. Children need to witness the frequency of change and struggle in their peers and in us. We can tell these nourishing stories.

Our community elders make natural griots—human repositories of oral history. Their life basket is full with stories of change, crisis, and triumph. Elders are a natural source of calm and perspective awaiting our young. By rupturing the extended family in society, we have greatly ruptured this relationship between the generations. In doing so, we have stolen a resource from our children.

An energy shift takes place between middle ages and elderhood, just as it does between childhood and adulthood. This shift often brings a tranquility born of perspective—an understanding of what we control and what we do not control. It is a letting go of old anxieties and self-imposed stress. Anxious youth seek this ground.

Children in turmoil are on a quest for calm places to rest, and good stories that help make sense of their lives. Our elders are yet another of the many resources nature provides toward this end. All we have to do is honor this relationship and facilitate the bonds.

We can facilitate storytelling throughout a child's social circles. Her own storytelling empowers and heals her as immediately as a loving embrace. When she shares, she feasts. Storytelling—historical and fictional—places her beside the parade of human possibility.

WORKING WISE

Children need stories. Stories create fertile flow. Children also need us to let go of our death grip on habit. Sometimes our habitual ways of relating to youth create dams that block the flow of understanding and intimacy. There is such a thing as trying too hard in the wrong way when trying less hard in the right way would be more prosperous. Many families beat their heads against the wall of their child's turmoil. They throw everything they can grasp from the closet of their own reality at the un-giving wall of child struggle. The wall does not break. Frustration and resentment settle into the families' hearts, subtle as heavy dust on a carpet. They blame the child for holding up the wall.

These parents have worked hard, but they have worked hard at burying their heads in the Earth of their own cultural reality. At some point they must unlash themselves from the restraints of their own reality and begin the earnest work of *voyaging* into their child's reality. This requires the often painful act of surrendering their sense of superiority as to how they see and live their lives.

This face-to-face with prejudice and nakedness is necessary in order to grow legs for walking around the wall of turmoil. Necessary so they can begin to glimpse the elusive jewel we call child.

ADULT-CHILD RELATIONSHIPS

The way in which we engage youth along the continuum of honor and condescension dictates virtually everything. The orientation of these relationships can be considered as: horizontal, vertical, interdependent, and fragmented. The implications of these orientations are vital in the home and in the school, in the community and in society.

In HORIZONTAL relationships, cultural awareness springs forth easily and naturally, with youth as a prominent source. Youth feel welcome and safe to respectfully express their truth within such a space. Adults and youth approach their relationship as a learning environment in which knowledge flows horizontally from and to each, not only from the adult. This horizontal plane does not require that we adults give up our authority. It means that our authority is compassionate—it seeks to understand and respond to need.

Each person is free and encouraged to judge the cultural integrity or heritage-honoring climate in the relationship. Culture and heritage are fragrances released into the relationship, integrated into shared habits and traditions. The fragrances are not fragmented inside the relationship or segregated from the center of the relationship. The sweetness pervades. Honoring children as equals opens us and them so they may enrich us with their lessons and we may receive them.

VERTICAL relationships are a traditional form in many cultures. Their effectiveness depends upon the degree of rigidity to the slope. In this alignment, the adult is the provider of knowledge and the child is the passive recipient. Knowledge and implicit values flow in one direction: downhill according to the slope created by the power-dominant adult. In this climate, not only does teaching flow in one exclusive direction, but cultural tone and insight tend to flow in one restricted direction as well. There is no two-way valve. Because the adult's cultural truth dominates, the child's truth is oppressed. Valuable cultural insight and sensitivities are lost.

Vertical relationships can be condescending and devaluing. When looking down the ladder we are liable to step on children because our feet are near their heads. Looking up the ladder they can only see our less flattering traits! Personal beauty flows best into us and out of us when we hold children as equals in spirit.

INTERDEPENDENT relationships take children into a space that encourages and celebrates mutuality and collective responsibility toward goals. Individual concerns are not neglected. Relational dynamics encourage a team spirit and shared vision. We reward children for investing themselves with a communal spirit. We show them how these relationships are productive and lead to their life success. In this climate, cultural wisdom and sensitivity within a child is more likely to be expressed and manifested, and in more productive ways.

A FRAGMENTED relationship invites children into ever-deepening pockets of isolation. Valuable relationship content rots and ferments. Years pass without any greater cultural insight into the child than when the relationship began. Child personal concerns, insults to spirit, and wounds are largely suppressed, either never to be aired, or ultimately vented in a counterproductive manner. In other words, the humanistic spirit is deleted from the software of "basic" information exchange!

Optimally, we should seek to create horizontal, interdependent relationships with our youth. Maximum flow in both directions results from optimal dilation of the valves between us, the valves that carry compassion, love, and understanding. This is how we fertilize honor.

HONORING RECONCILIATION

Every relationship requires continual reconciliation: the act of honest reckoning. One principle that Mohandas K. Gandhi prescribed for honorable human relations is the appreciation of differences. Here, people move beyond simply accepting others and achieve a genuine appreciation for their way of being human.

In a kindred spirit, Martin Luther King, Jr. designated six steps necessary on the path of social change: information gathering; education; personal commitments; negotiation; direct action; and reconciliation and beginning the healing process. These steps equally apply to our relationships with youth.

The last step in Dr. King's process, reconciliation, is perhaps the most neglected in relationships. Because of this, children suffer from a lack of testimony as to their woundedness. In the ways that they are wounded by us or in relationship with us, we are responsible for engaging together with them in a process of healing.

True reconciliation is a stream of elements: testimony, acknowledgement, apology, forgiveness, and shared commitment to change. These are the seeds of healing and union. Testimony is achieved when children are encouraged to freely, honestly share their wound-story with us. As they share, they require that we clearly acknowledge receiving what they share. If they do not feel we are listening with genuine focus and compassion, they experience their testimony as a farce.

When we apologize for the hurt a child sees us as the source of, we offer partial proof that we have truly listened. Our opinion of our role in her pain is not the focus here. When we defend ourselves, minimize her hurt, or attack what she has said we have just destroyed the path toward reconciliation. All that matters in this process is that we apologize for the hurt she says we have caused.

Genuine apology makes her feel that we care about her feelings. It opens the door for the next step: forgiveness. We cannot expect her to forgive us if she feels that we have not even recognized how we are harming her. The initiation of her forgiveness is our responsibility. We have to make our humility clear to her. Even if we do not yet understand how we might have hurt her, we let her know that we are devoted to understanding.

This devotion is part of the step that follows: a shared commitment to change. It is likely that our wounded child has wounded us. This is the nature of woundedness. We both require the validation of our wounds. Once we both have had the opportunity for validated testimony, we will have created the grounds for true healing and a repaired relationship. Reconciliation can be very challenging in a relationship full of anger, blame, and criticism habits. Adults and children need to patiently build safe spaces for this kind of shared work. One day at a time we find the courage and trust to begin. As we progress we realize we are dosing ourselves with holistic medicine, the most powerful medicine of all.

HOLISTIC MEDICINE

In the pristine mountain air above the clouds, Tibetan doctors receive their patients. *Patience.* These healers practice patience. Symptoms are not their concern. They open up the moment for the patient to tell her story. The doctor is interested in the life that has brought her here.

The doctor's medicine is gathered and ground directly from nature. The herbs have no interest in the patient's symptoms. They are percolating to be released into the root of her ailment. She tells this healer who she is, who is in her life, where she has been, what she has seen. She describes her diet, her dreams, her fears, her family. A portrait is being painted of what has touched her life.

This kind of doctoring takes time. This health seeking requires an allowance for true healing and life changes. Healing is a well-cultivated blossom in the intertwined hands of the healer and his charge. Trust lines the space in which they meet. No one is rushed. No symptoms are bandaged. The patient is allowed to testify on her behalf.

Once the source of ailment has been discovered the prescription is for the life space the patient inhabits. Her case is not treated as an individual case but rather as treatment of collective lives. If the conditions of her life that produced the illness are not transformed, her illness cannot be transformed. With diligence the healer leads her down her path toward well-being. Having located and treated the root, recurrence is unlikely. Both parties ultimately save time and money—the cycle of sickness has been broken. There will be no repeat visits.

We must treat the root. When a child has been called names and attacked at school, it is important that we directly bolster the part of her that has been devalued. Vague comments about how she is a wonderful person and should ignore ignorance do not salve her wound. Holistic medicine demands that we leave our symptom-stroking alone and treat her wound.

We have it in us to be this way, searching out child stories to find the root. For the young all that is required is that they be themselves and speak the truth. For us, faith that true understanding is worth the wait.

FEEDING CATTLE

Have you heard the story about the rancher who wanted to fatten his cattle before market? He was a good, intelligent man. He continued to give his cattle their usual feed. Each day he placed them on the scale. Each day their weight remained the same. He became frustrated with this lack of growth. One early morning his young son, wiping his sleepy eyes, came out to the pasture to greet him. He noticed his father's frustration and wished to help. In the cool air of sunrise he asked his father a simple question: *Daddy, if you want to make your cows grow, why don't you just feed them better food?*

A rancher's revelation was born that day: Weighing cattle does not make them heavier. At some point, if you want cattle to grow, you have to feed them sufficiently. This is a lesson for us. If we want children to learn, we have to teach them. Excessive testing at best produces test-taking skills. True learning requires us to provide true teaching. We have to educate, according to the uniqueness of child learning styles, culture, and life experiences.

If we want our children to be filled with pride in their whole, we have to put pride into them. We have to stroke and celebrate their true beauty. Constantly telling them to have pride in who they are without infusing them with the ingredients for pride produces very little.

If our goal is for them to become forgiving, they require that we pour our forgiveness into them. Certainly if we yearn for their respect, nature dictates that we penetrate them with our own respect. Farmers, ranchers, people whose lives depend on getting things to grow, become devoted only to providing the appropriate nutrition. This is an attitude for us to model. No more labels for categorizing our young according to their struggles. Only what they need to grow.

CELEBRATING YOUR SELF

Those who serve and raise children are under-valued by society in many ways. This leaves them carrying the burden of forces that can have destructive impact. Celebrating our selves counteracts harmful factors and increases personal and professional well-being.

Stress-reducing activities allow us to celebrate who we are and the tasks at hand. Each moment can become a stress release valve if we create strong mental habits. Journaling and other expressive exercises create those habits and critical awareness of our internal state.

Creative self-expression of any kind is a celebration. The more avenues we can find for our personal and professional voice, the more exuberant our celebration.

Many of us have two resources that we tend to under-utilize. Our professional life exists as a resource that can empower our personal life. All we need to do is to develop the habit of taking stock of the lessons and people we experience in our professional life. Even the negative moments can be siphoned for positive insight. Our own behavior, attitudes, and reactions at work are insights for how we can, or should not, exist outside of work.

Once we have gathered our treasure chest of lessons, we can take it home and open it up there. A good treasure chest will release a vibrant scent through the household. Everyone who lives there benefits.

The second resource we have is our personal life. Everything that it offers us we may find a way to translate into strengths and resources for our professional life.

Becoming brazen promoters of success is a celebratory act. Success exists all around us and in us. All we need to do is publicize it. We, our family, our colleagues, and clients form a single team, though we may not realize it. Publicizing successes, small and large, of any team member is a way of celebrating our self as an extension of that team. Focusing on our small accomplishments moves us steadily into larger achievements.

We also benefit when we become adept at expressing appreciation to everyone on our team, including to self. Expressing appreciation is like watering plants except that everyone who expresses appreciation has a green thumb. Whoever we water with appreciation is filled with undeniable warmth. No one resents being appreciated. Relationships are strengthened this way. Morale is lifted— the emotional confetti of a true celebration.

Since we exist as teams regardless of our awareness or desire to be a team, team-building should be a part of our celebration. We can work on our communication, role clarity, processes, and objectives. Our positive collective identity celebrates our individual identity and vice versa.

Most of all we celebrate by nurturing our body, mind, heart, and spirit. Our parts work in tandem. What parts we strengthen, strengthen the whole. Each part has its own unique nature while also existing in concert with the nature of the other parts. Learning how to nurture our entire system is like planning a party. Good things come from putting the pieces in place.

HELP THE CHILD BY HELPING YOUR SELF

Much of how we enrich a young man emerges from how we enrich our self. Increasing our cultural competency with him is a good start. This means that we make the effort to learn the full expanse of how he exists in the world: his values, sensitivities, fears, passions, dreams—all of him. As we go on this voyage we are forced to examine our prejudices, which we can conceive as the roadblocks to our knowing of him. Our prejudices are the thistles and thorns in our embrace of him.

Part of the work order is that we make an effort to clarify and broaden our identity. The clearer we are in seeing self the clearer we see him. Vision is a looking glass that works both ways. Polish one side of the glass and we shine the other. As we stabilize our identity by extending ourselves into the wholeness of our life, we develop a respect for the idea of cultural integrity. We understand how precious our own way of living is to us. This creates a compassionate protectiveness in honoring the way in which he lives.

On our path toward growth we explore our deeper motivations and attitudes. We delve far into the soil of our being, uncovering the roots of our thoughts, feelings, and behavior. Our self-discovery leads to increased esteem and confidence. From our nest of security, we become less fixated on fixing him and more focused on knowing him.

We inspect our patterns of communication and reaction. A person unaware of the hammer lashed to her tongue cannot know when she is battering others. We take stock in our anxiety and nervousness. The best way to raise a neurotic child is to bathe him in our own fears and worries daily. His emotional skin will wrinkle and prune in that water. He will have learned from us that life is to be dealt with nervously. This is how fragility tiptoes through the generations.

The formula is astounding in its simplicity. What we work to become dominates his becoming. We have a greater power than we know. We do not even have to be his parent to exert such influence. Children's lives have been changed by the beneficent stroke of a single behavior witnessed, and by a singular word or conversation. He rides in our leaky boat across his unsure ocean of days. We help him the most when we bail our own water.

BUILDING RELATIONSHIPS

We have the creative capacity to develop exercises, rituals, and habits that serve as the foundation of our whole identity. This is how we build our relationships, including the all-important relationship with self. We can include children, family, and colleagues in these activities. Here are a few exercises from which we can build:

JOURNALING. Life's fullness can easily dislodge us from our path. Keeping a written or mental journal can help preserve our identity as a parent or child advocate. Identity is a habit, a repetition of thoughts defining the self. The more often we exercise this identity check the more clarity and stability we achieve. Here are some self-defining questions we can journal:

Why did I choose to be a parent/advocate? What are my goals in this role? How do I wish to improve? What are my values in this role? How is this role a part of my personal growth and well-being?

How are each of my actions and attitudes serving the needs of the child, and each member of the circle? How can I improve each? How can I gain cultural competence?

How can I resolve conflict with circle members? How can I manage my role-related stress? How can my personal life empower my role? How are my personal experiences, challenges, and strengths influencing the child?

We can always look to others for the answers to these questions. But the most valuable answers come from within. Child-honoring behaviors and attitudes are primarily functions of personal desire, commitment, and creativity, not knowledge or education. More precisely, we honor children through good old-fashioned hard work at creating honorable habits. We each are unique individuals serving uniquely under unique circumstances. Honorable child relations are the result of fully tapping into our instinct, intuition, and experiences to create a personal portrait of integrity.

CULTURAL ASSESSMENT. To be aware of how our way of being might affect a child and her way of being, we need to assess our cultural reality. This is a process of examining our values, beliefs, sensitivities, traditions, inclinations, fears, hopes, presumptions. It is an interview we hold with ourselves about the entirety of who we are. The more we can create a written portrait of our way of being, the more self-awareness we generate. We can share our assessment with others close to us to gain valuable feedback on our view of self. This should be an ongoing evaluation. Our cultural reality is fluid and ever-changing.

Our motivations for being in a child's life influence our entire relationship. It is crucial that we be entirely aware of those motivations. Do we have the courage to be honest? If not, what can we do to increase our courage? Very rarely do we have a single motivation. It is more likely that we carry several reasons. And it is highly possible that our motives are a mixture of admirable and less admirable traits. Those less attractive motives are the ones we need to unearth and be honest with ourselves about, if not also with the child. Motives are the hidden land mines and gold mines in our relationship together. Uncovering both is essential.

RECKONING WITH OUR PREJUDICES. Prejudices are a natural consequence of being socialized by the values of family, community, and society. Our personal prejudices play a significant role in our capacity to operate at our optimal level. Those prejudices that relate to the heritage and culture of a child are of particular concern. Being honest with self about possible prejudices is the first step toward fully accessing our child-honoring toolbox. This toolbox holds our gifts of intuition, creativity, compassion, empathy, assessment, problem-solving, and relationship-building. Prejudice is rust on the lock.

BE IMPERFECT. We need to breathe. Our self-imposed perfection expectation regarding our performance with children leads to defensiveness and control orientation. This is perfection paralysis. Everyone benefits when we allow ourselves to be flawed, incomplete beings in progress, just as children are. Young people aren't the only ones who wear masks. Ours are often masks of perfection. Allowing imperfection is not an excuse for failing to grow. It simply lifts the weight of undue expectation as we grow.

GRATITUDE AND APPRECIATION. Raising and serving children are high stress, low resource, low social reward occupations. In these endeavors, criticizing children becomes the easiest reflex for releasing steam and expressing oneself. Simply by writing weekly or monthly notes of appreciation or gratitude to children can work wonders for our relationships with them. Expressing appreciation can become a strong foundational trait within a family culture. When we model this behavior for children it becomes their own positive social skill.

Even in the most friction-heavy relationships, try to reflect on the other person's positive attributes. Then simply list those qualities on a sheet of paper with the heading being something such as: *I appreciate you for* . . . . Give your note to her or leave it for her if that is more comfortable to you. We can do this for whatever relationship brings us stress or conflict. The more consistently we do this the more our relationships flower.

One of our most rewarding practices can be that of expressing appreciation. When we share with a child what it is we appreciate about him, he is showered in affirmation. We have just dropped him a hint as to how he belongs as a part of our life. Our appreciation is his membership card. This habit goes a long way to calming conflict and anger and creating esteem. We earn our advanced degree when we learn to identify traits worth appreciating that are not so obvious. When we learn to express appreciation even as we discipline we are on to something. This makes discipline more effective. It opens a child for the seed of our lesson to be planted.

LOVE LETTERS. All children, but especially those who have experienced dislocation, separation, and loss, require constant reaffirmation that they are loved. In addition to verbalizing this to them, try writing them love letters. Think of all a child's beauty. Write it into a love note. Fold it up. Tuck it in his notebook before school, or after a disappointment. Pray that he will open it, swallow the words, and open up, a blossom stroked by your loving sun.

He can collect these notes and treasure them for rainy days and moments when he struggles. Tell him what your love for him does for you, and how much you value his love for you. Loving is a skill and therefore is built upon loving habits. Teach him this habit and he will reciprocate your love in plenitude.

PEACE NOTES. These are letters we write to self. When we are feeling hurt, betrayed, or taken for granted, we are simply experiencing woundedness to our own child within. This child remains with us forever. It is important to directly embrace these feelings and then nurture them. Literally write to your own feelings and let it be known that you understand; that it is going to be all right; that the person who hurt you was acting out of his own suffering or misunderstanding. We need to talk and write ourselves into a place of peace. It takes practice and regularity but will immeasurably benefit our children and social circle.

CELEBRATE UNIQUENESS. We can use each family or team member's natural uniqueness as a cause for celebration rather than as something to avoid. Any trait within the realms of personal heritage and culture is worthy of our celebration. Together we can learn to associate differences as a trigger for positive reactions such as appreciation and learning.

IMAGINE SEPARATION. This exercise can help us to understand what it means to be acutely separated from family: Write down the names of 10 of the people who mean the most to you in your life. Now describe in writing exactly what these people mean to you. Next, honestly imagine and describe how you would be affected by losing every one of these people, all at once. Please do not run away from this thought if it frightens you. A doorway stands before you. On the other side, potentially, is your relationship with an uprooted child, changed.

Describe in detail the impact on you, through genuine contemplation of how you would be impacted by the unique loss of each person. Magnify this impact by the degree of the sensitivity, need, and vulnerability you recall having as a child. Finally, imagine and describe what it would take for you to heal from such a separation and become whole and thriving. If you can remain fully present and honest through this exercise, you may achieve a priceless revelation about separation, and about yourself.

COMPASSIONATE LISTENING. This may require extensive practice, as do most child-honoring skills. When a child is expressing herself to us, it is critical that we listen with our total being. What is often most critical to her is feeling that she is truly being heard and understood. Avoid interruptions, judgment, advice, and negative nonverbal expressions. She will learn to feel safe sharing with us as we receive all she has to share. And as we do so with openness and complete devotion to understanding.

LOVING SPEECH. In every communication, including those involving disciplining a child, we can learn to impart a message that we love her. Loving speech constantly seeks to validate her, reassure her, and empower her. It is not demeaning, spiteful, manipulative, or controlling. It is compassionate and full of faith in her even when it is necessary to be firm or corrective.

PLEDGES OF HONOR. Although we are adults, we still carry with us the habit of punishing those who disappoint us. We do this through subtle and obvious behavior and nonverbal communication. More productive is the practice of identifying those factors that led to the disappointment. Then together we can create simple, mutually binding pledges for the relationship. These one-page signed agreements spell out what both parties pledge to do and not do to achieve success together in the relationship.

These simple, social oaths can effectively create behavior and attitude change. Pledges ideally should be posted visibly and reviewed regularly.

PERSONAL COMPASS. Create your own personal compass, which is a written pledge you make to yourself. This pledge reminds you of who you are; presents your values clearly; and dictates how you will strive to respond in various social situations. Create a positive, self-affirming personal compass and use it as an exercise in clear identity. This is how we can learn to direct ourselves through challenging moments. This is how we remain anchored in a healthy place of mind and heart.

GIVE A GIFT WHEN ANGRY. Give a gift to someone, anyone! Their appreciation at receiving your gift can help melt away anger you are feeling. Especially if the gift requires thoughtfulness. This will distract you from your anger and shift you into a positive focus. Giving pacifies.

APOLOGIZE SINCERELY. When someone feels hurt by us, ultimately what matters is not that their hurt is justified. That is not for us to judge. For the relationship to move forward in a healthy manner, we should apologize sincerely for having caused the wound. Doing so, we instantly create a level of trust that would not exist if we did not stop to validate the other person's feelings.

VENTING IS NOT HEALING. Venting our anger is simply a rehearsal of our anger. Our anger does not diminish. It grows stronger just like the muscle that we have exercised. Catharsis is a myth when it comes to expressing ourselves angrily in an attempt to lose our anger. We must acknowledge and understand our anger, and then work at healing the true root of it. That root often is not what a person recently did to us to trigger our anger. The root usually is a deeper wound that has made us more sensitive to certain triggers.

NO ENEMIES. Practice telling yourself each and every day that you have no enemies in this world. Rather that the people who hurt you have done so because they are suffering themselves or because they have misunderstood something. Practice just like you once practiced tying your shoes as a child. Now you think nothing of tying your shoes. It comes naturally. Your brain has to grow accustomed to this idea of *No Enemies* before it can become reflexive. Perceiving no enemies grants us access to peace. If we perceive enemies everywhere, we will always be on guard, tense, closed, stressed. Having no enemies is a joyful place to occupy, once we make the trek.

SEEDS OF COMPASSION. Regularly monitor your true thoughts and your actions and ask yourself: *Am I watering the seeds of my compassion or the seeds of my anger?* Whatever it is that you give your time, attention, and energy will grow from seed to sprout to stalk and eventually to a full grown living thing. Whether you produce a beautiful shade tree or an ugly ominous cloud depends on which seeds you water. Another way to think of it: Are you watering your inner flowers or your inner weeds? If you wish to cultivate beauty, then water beauty in your thoughts, actions, and words. If you wish to cultivate ugly, the seeds of your weeds are already within you!

WRITE A BOOK ON YOURSELF. This can be a great way to get to know yourself; to discover the roots of your pain and your passions; to heal yourself; to clarify your identity; to become centered; and to discover a whole new season of life. You do not have to exclusively use words.

Painting, drawing, photos, and scraps are available to you. Even if you never show anyone the book or leave it as a gift for your children or loved ones it is well worth the effort. The truest value in a book for the author is in the experience of contemplation and discovery during the production. Sprinkle it with humor, poetry, philosophy, imagery, whatever you wish—this is your opportunity to make a beautiful portrait with the colors of your life. Paint freely like you did when you were a child!

KNOW YOUR SELF. Identity serves as a compass guiding us through our role in a child's life. Our clarity about who we are in his life improves our discernment, instincts, and decision-making. Identity is also a scale that dictates the value we assign to ourselves: The greater the value, the lesser our insecurities. This provides for our stability and his. Because of these implications, it is vital that we develop a whole identity.

Doing so enriches us with an array of benefits, including purpose and vision; esteem and self-worth; self-security and stress relief; motivation and morale; improved problem-solving and crisis resolution; increased creativity and insight; healthier relationships; self-validation; balance and centeredness; stronger voice; courage and confidence; and ultimately the kind of entrenched peace that comes from enduring faith in self.

Search. Search for your truth. Venture to the corners of your farthest hollows. Peel back the layers of avoidance that have pushed you away from your core. Do this for yourself, not only for our children.

Know your self. This is a mantra we can offer ourselves and our young. Knowing your self is the first step in being true to your self. It is the key to self-determination. A child cannot become self-healing without first knowing her self. This knowledge shines a light on her personal inventory of resources. Through reflection, exploration, and creative expression a young boy begins his reunion with self. The world has taken him so far away. He has all the tools to return. He has every reason to return. By knowing his self he acquires the key to his living. Our path is the same. The destination is a delta we call peace.

REMEMBERING PEACE

When an animal and a child meet in nature they hold a private conversation. The animal looks the child in the eyes and asks, "Why are you so nervous inside your own skin? This is not your nature. I remember when you were newborn and fully present in every moment, not scattered and skittish."

The child, staring back, says, "You remind me of how I used to be."

The animal replies, "What happened to you?"

The child answers, "I am surrounded by all these nervous adults. Eventually, before I knew it, I had joined them in their dance."

Children are not yet so departed from the brilliant calm of nature that when they meet a wild animal they cannot remember peace.

We carry an energy field around with us. Our family projects an energy field. Our community is an energy field. Children have no choice but to swim in this. Many children, traumatized by separation, are nervous already. Now we embrace them nervously because truthfully we are afraid of what they represent to us. Now we are nervous people making nervous children more nervous!

So much of their chance to breathe deeply and finally relax depends on us breathing and relaxing. Our work is to create relaxing spaces. Otherwise we are creating neurotic spaces, and then talking with each other about finding therapy for children who seem to be acting neurotically. We need to laugh more as part of loving them.

TEMPLES FOR THE CHILD SOUL

We have spent these many years in society building homes for children; structures of wood and stone filled with caregivers laden of love and skills and resources. It is time now for us to build temples for the child soul. Thus we begin to fill these yearning youthful vessels with the substance that will deliver them unto their own divine potential. Temples flowing with streams of validation, confirmation, and celebration, where the faucets run with sweet water and the basins fill into clear reflection ponds.

The Sufi poet Hafiz wrote: *The great artist no longer hurts himself or anyone and keeps on sculpting light.* We can be that great presence in the lives of our children. They are available to us to sculpt, though their ultimate form is beyond our imagination. Their ultimate form is a dream that Creation dreams. Let's no longer hurt ourselves or any child and keep on sculpting light.

These children have not become less
they have become more
they have been carved deeper
seen farther
touched a real place that exists
beyond togetherness

their tongues have tasted fragmentation
and come up spitting

in that valley of bitterness
their spirits strong
their roots forge deep
until they taste the sweeter river seep

and there a stand is made
refusing to exit grand parade
young trumpets blaring
tender hearts daring
to do some caring

when sadness creeps across their face
can we at least allow them
that simple human grace
sign of the life that has come as cloud

and now their song sung out loud
and we the canyon catching
that glinted glory
bow before the Greater Good
wrapped in story
of how a child could
walk in shadows
be set a-sail
yet still find peace
inside life's curling veil.

Fawn nestles under a proud oak tree, sleeping. Her dreams are of the clear, calm water. In ethereal imagining, all the sunlight of her life gathers in that magical pond. Her sleeping heart beats, light, content. She is *shanti ko samjhana*. She is remembering peace.

GRATITUDE

To my Creator . . . Ashé. For my ancestors who beat a persistent drum inside my heart. Keep the drum alive so that I may locate you in this Endless Sky. To the children of separation: I pray that I have served you.

To my beloved daughter, for swelling my heart. To all of my parents, I am the glint from your precious gemstones. With me you have set many fires! Keesha, your love, support, patience, and faith in me allowed this book to come. My family and friends, I surrender my heart to those of you who truly *see* me. Dita, thank you for the last-minute save!

Eric, since our days in Manzanita dorm your friendship has brought wondrous designs to the canvass of my living. Thanks for the great artwork for this book. Jackie, you soulful butterfly. My words fly free because of your editorial vision. Char, my friend, it has been 22 years now of intoxicating ourselves on laughter. Thank you for your love and generous offering of your editing precision. Kent, my loyal leaning tree. Thanks for your eagle eye on these pages!

Barbara, I have been blessed to walk on Earth in your time. Thank you, friend, for inviting me into the heart of your Pueblo people. Yeshashwork, I am grateful for your loyal, playful spirit and unique insight on the separation journey. Marilynn B. Brewer, for her theoretical work on *optimal distinctiveness.* Signithia Fordham and John U. Ogbu, for their empirical exploration of *oppositional identity.*

For the incandescent lanterns who swam in the side streams and created divine waves for us to ride: Mohandas K. Gandhi, Martin Luther King, Jr., Harriet Tubman, Chief Seathl (Seattle), Chief Crow, Thich Nhat Hanh (still swimming!), Hafiz, and Rumi. The words on this page are the crumbs of my gratitude. In my living I serve the feast.

INDEX OF STREAMS

Jaiya John lives in Silver Spring, Maryland. He is blessed with the beauty of his daughter and serves his life mission through writing, speaking, and mentoring. He breathes poetry and dreams of human freedom. He is the founder and executive director of Soul Water Rising, a human relations mission stirring the soul to remember itself.

R. Eric Stone created the cover design for this book as well as the whole identity graphic and Soul Water Rising logo. He is a scenic designer and educator in theatre and a graphic designer. www.rericstone.com.

Other Books by Jaiya John

To learn more about this and other books by Jaiya John, to order bulk quantities, or to learn about Soul Water Rising's global human relations work, please visit us at: www.soulwater.org.

Soul Water Rising chooses to not use endorsement statements in its books.

WWW.SOULWATER.ORG
WWW.JAIYAJOHN.COM

CPSIA information can be obtained at www.ICGtesting.com
Printed in the USA
BVOW05s0459050215

386429BV00004B/13/P